THE Justin Bieber ALBUM

GARRETT BALDWIN

Plexus, London

For Brian Krajack

All rights reserved including the right
of reproduction in whole or in part in any form
Copyright © 2010 by Garrett Baldwin
Published by Plexus Publishing Limited
25 Mallinson Road
London SW11 1BW
www.plexusbooks.com

British Library Cataloguing in Publication Data

Baldwin, Garrett.
    The Justin Bieber album.
    1. Bieber, Justin, 1994–Juvenile literature.
    2. Singers–Canada–Biography–Juvenile literature.
    I. Title
    782.4'2166'092-dc22

    ISBN-13: 978-0-85965-464-7
    ISBN-10: 0-85965-464-8

Front cover photo by Dan Hallman/Corbis Outline
Back cover photo by Anthony Cutajar/Retna Ltd/Corbis
Cover and book design by Coco Wake-Porter
Printed in China by Imago

Acknowledgements
The author would like to thank the Weinig family, Sandra Wake,
Coco Wake-Porter, Laura Coulman and Tom Branton for their
tireless efforts at Plexus. This book clearly would not have been done
without all of your hard work. A special thank you is also extended
to Jay Soderberg and Mike Hochhauser.

    Justin Bieber has given innumerable interviews to newspapers,
magazines, websites, television and radio. The author and editors
would like to give special thanks to the following: *Rolling Stone,
New York Times, Entertainment Weekly, Chicago Tribune, Chicago
Sun-Times, Toronto Star, Washington Post, Boston Globe, Telegraph,
J-14, Twist, Maxim, New York Post, Vancouver Sun, Press Association,
Associated Press, Minneapolis Star Tribune, Baltimore Sun, Herald Sun,*
abh-news.com, mtv.com, billboard.com, crushable.com,
justinbieber.com, welcometostratford.com, cnn.com, msnbc.com,
mlb.com, facebook.com, allmusic.com, usher.com, espn.com,
bet.com, hiphoprx.com, j-bieber.org, imdb.com, funnyordie.com,
justinbiebermusic.com, clevvertv.com, twitter.com, myspace.com,
prlog.org, neonlimelight.com, artistdirect.com, eonline.com,
gather.com, imnotobsessed.com, thehollywoodgossip.com,
poponthepop.com, starpulse.com, nydailynews.com, jam.canoe.ca,
news.bbc.co.uk/cbbcnews, disneydreaming.com, blogs.wsj.com,
mybliss.co.uk, etonline.com, capitalfm.com, summerfest.com,
watchmojo.com, q100atlanta.com, teentoday.co.uk, *ABC News, The
Oprah Winfrey Show, The Tonight Show with Jay Leno, CBS News,
MTV News, MTV Diary of Justin Bieber, The Zone, RTL News, CTV
W5, @katiecouric, Saturday Night Live, The Ellen DeGeneres Show,
The Today Show, Live with Regis and Kelly, Chelsea Lately, Access
Hollywood,* RadioLIVE, MuchMusic, Radio Now 100.9/IMC (Indie
Music Channel). *Justin Bieber (Get the Scoop)* by Ronny Bloom;
100% Justin Bieber: The Unofficial Biography by Evie Parker.

    We would also like to thank the following for supplying
photographs: Mike Coppola/FilmMagic/Getty Images; Anthony
Cutajar/Retna Ltd/Corbis; Michael N. Todaro/WireImage/Getty
Images; Theo Wargo/WireImage/Getty Images; Theo Wargo/
WireImage/Getty Images; Theo Wargo/WireImage/Getty Images;
Mike Stobe/Stringer/Getty Images Entertainment; Derek Storm/
Retna Ltd/Corbis; Noel Vasquez/Getty Images Entertainment; Kevin
Mazur/WireImage/Getty Images; Ben Meadows/WireImage/Getty;
Larry Busacca/Getty Images; Matthew Imaging/WireImage/Getty
Images; Kevin Winter/DCNYRE2010/Getty Images Entertainment;
Tim Mosenfelder/Getty Images; Michael Tran/FilmMagic/Getty
Images; James Devaney/WireImage/Getty Images; Jason LaVeris/
FilmMagic/Getty Images; Andrew H. Walker/Getty Images
Entertainment; Jeff Kravitz/FilmMagic/Getty Images;
Andrew H. Walker/Getty Images Entertainment; Kevin Mazur/
WireImage/Getty Images; Frank Micelotta/Getty Images
Entertainment; Christopher Polk/Getty Images Entertainment; Kevin
Mazur/WireImage/Getty Images; Dave Hogan/Stringer/Getty Images
Entertainment; Kevin Mazur/WireImage/Getty Images; Newspix/
Getty Images; Noel Vasquez/Getty Images Entertainment; George
Pimentel/WireImage/Getty Images; George Pimentel/WireImage/
Getty Images ; Larry Busacca/Getty Images Entertainment; Kevin
Winter/DCNYRE2010/Getty Images Entertainment; C. Flanigan/
FilmMagic/Getty Images; Ron Veseley/Getty Images Sport; George
Pimentel/WireImage/Getty Images; Jun Sato/WireImage/Getty
Images; Andy Sheppard/Redferns/Getty Images; Handout/Getty
Images Entertainment; C. Brandon/Redferns/Getty Images; Janette
Pellegrini/WireImage/Getty Images.

    Every effort has been made to acknowledge and trace copyright
holders and to contact original sources, and we apologise for any
unintentional errors which will be corrected in future editions.

Contents

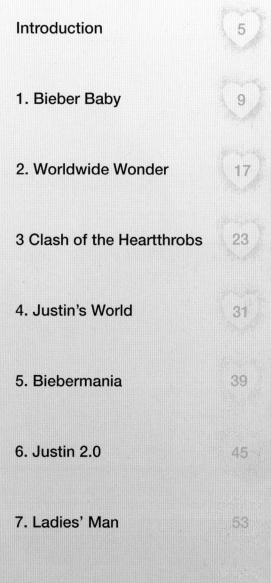

Introduction

'It's been pretty amazing and I'm really glad that I've just been able to do what I love.'

— Justin Bieber

Picture the scene: it's a gorgeous afternoon. And who better to spend it with than all your best girlfriends? Well, there is one name that springs to mind, along with a pair of hazel eyes and a voice as sweet as honey. *That* voice. You can hear it now, crooning out a promise to give you everything you need. The song is 'One Time' by Justin Bieber, of course. Though, actually, you've played it over and over, memorizing every last note. Lucky CDs don't wear out – except that this isn't a CD at all. It's not a recording and it's not just in your head. With a jolt, you realise that this truly is Justin Bieber – in the flesh and in your own backyard (could he be trampling your mom's prized plants with those bright purple trainers? Can you bring yourself to care?). You hear his fingers catch as he softly strums the guitar strings. And when he's singing about his 'shawty,' hand on heart, intense hazel gaze fixed on you alone, it feels as though you're the only two people in the garden – and quite possibly the world!

And so comes the point when it's customary for you to wake up. Except that, for two lucky girls the dream came true when they each purchased one half of Justin Bieber's two-part debut album to find a shining golden ticket inside. The prize in this contest? A private concert in their backyard performed by none other than the pop icon himself. Justin's golden ticket contest drew thousands and thousands of fans to stores, hopeful that this incredible prize could be theirs. Millions of copies of Justin's two-part debut album, *My World* and *My World 2.0*, were sold, but only two records contained the tickets that provided the lucky fans in question with their once-in-a-lifetime experience.

It was no surprise that so many fans flocked for their chance to win a private concert with Justin. At the age of sixteen, Justin Bieber is the most in-demand music entertainer in the world today. With two platinum-selling albums and a six-month North American tour underway,

Justin poses at the Empire State Building in New York, as part of Jumpstart's Fourth Annual National Read for the Record Day, October 2009.

Justin's star is certainly on the rise. But one of the most incredible aspects of his story is that just three years ago, very few people had any idea who he was. In that time, Justin has gone from strumming his acoustic guitar on the streets of Stratford, Ontario to playing in front of a sold-out crowd at Madison Square Garden. A song-and-dance showman who plays four different instruments, Justin's rise to global stardom is an incredible story that began with him broadcasting his remarkable self-taught talents on YouTube for fun and led to the emergence of a teenage pop star who has sold out practically every stop of his summer 2010 tour.

What separates Justin Bieber from past and current teen icons is that he is a naturally gifted singer-songwriter of remarkable maturity and, more importantly, his rise to fame is directly linked to the enthusiasm generated by his fans, many of whom found him before he inked his first record deal. Millions of fans now monitor his every word on Twitter and Facebook, while some men in New York have paid hundreds of dollars to high-priced salons in order to mimic his signature mop-top hairstyle, aptly named 'The Bieber.'

Unlike the talented singers and actors who have worked exclusively with Disney, Justin Bieber stands alone as the first amateur YouTube sensation to reach international superstardom by acquiring a global fan base that spans generations and gender lines. While Disney-endorsed performers like Miley Cyrus, Demi Lovato, and the Jonas Brothers still dominate the pop genre, all three acts pale in comparison to the phenomenally hyped young man commonly known as 'Biebs.'

Since he began his singing career by posting amateur performances of his favorite songs online three years ago, Justin has developed a massive fan base and achieved international stardom. By the time he was accidentally discovered by his current manager Scooter Braun on YouTube in 2008, Justin (with his web-savvy mother's assistance) had already built a dynamic, cult-like following, and was ranked the number one most-subscribed-to musician in Canada before he ever agreed to his first album deal. His first meeting with his eventual mentor, the immensely talented producer and singer Usher Raymond, was a forgettable experience that later led to a second chance and his life-changing audition in Atlanta, Georgia.

Since becoming the first musician ever to have an incredible seven songs from his debut album chart simultaneously on *Billboard*'s Hot 100, Justin has broken record after record, while the more than 165 million views of his performances on YouTube accumulated in the past three years speak volumes about his worldwide appeal. Today he remains one of the most subscribed-to musicians on the web and continues to interact with 2.5 million fans every day via Twitter and Facebook.

But Justin still finds himself starry-eyed when he's in the same room as celebrity royalty, even though he has now performed for the President of the United States and was one of the youngest musical guests in the history of *Saturday Night Live*. Touring the globe with his mother, manager and 'swagger coach,' Justin shows no signs of slowing down. A remarkable self-trained musician, his beginnings were humble: a young kid who survived the tragedy of family separation and found himself playing music on the streets of Stratford, an extraordinary talent who continues to evolve. From his foot-fracturing performance at Wembley Arena to his record-breaking album sales, Justin is now a humble superstar whose mother resides at the center of his world, and will be one of the hottest tickets in the music industry for years to come. 'It's been pretty amazing and I'm really glad that I've just been able to do what I love,' Bieber told CNN while on tour in 2010. 'I'm really glad that I get to travel the world and, like I said, "Just do what I love to do."'

'How you doin'?' The Biebs smolders for the camera in New York, May 2009.

1

Bieber Baby

'Oh yeah, for sure – I love my mom!'
– Justin Bieber

Any impassioned Biebette who has ever dreamed of dropping by the tiny apartment where Justin first developed his sweet, soulful voice would do well to wear a winter coat and – unless they're lucky enough to live there already – buy themselves a plane ticket to Canada. That's because Justin Drew Bieber was born in Stratford, Ontario on 1 March 1994, the only child of Pattie and Jeremy Bieber. Having married in their late teens, both parents were eager to share the joyful news of their first child's arrival with their friends and family. A tiny baby with mousy chestnut hair and deep brown eyes, Justin was healthy and happy in his mother's arms on the day of his birth. It would be the first of many loving days and nights spent with his mom.

Stratford itself is a quiet little city nestled on the Avon River, approximately two hours southwest of Toronto, Ontario. Named after the birthplace of the world-famous playwright William Shakespeare, the town was originally built as a connection point for the Canadian National Railroad. Founded as a town in 1859, Stratford became a city seven years later and, after more than 150 years, its population has grown to over 30,000. Growing up in Stratford, Justin's dreams might have been filled with stage lights and screaming fans, but in reality, he doubted that any resident of his hometown had ever achieved any level of fame. 'Nothing ever came out of Stratford,' Justin admits. 'It's almost an impossible dream that you just don't think about.' But Justin was wrong to think this way. He certainly wasn't the first resident of his hometown to make a name for himself. Actor Shawn Roberts, singer Loreena McKennitt, and Canadian news anchor Tony Parsons have all lived in Stratford. Opera singers James Westman and Roger Honeywell, and former NHL hockey player Tim Taylor also made their homes in the Bieb's backyard. And Justin would certainly never have been able to sing along to his favorite tunes in front of the mirror while brushing his teeth if it hadn't been for Thomas Edison. Edison, who invented the light bulb and the record player, once

Breaking hearts before breakfast: Justin gives the nation a taste of Bieber Fever
while performing on Good Morning America *in November 2009.*

worked as a telegraph operator for the Grand Trunk Railway at Stratford's train station. Stratford has had more than its share of resident go-getters over the years.

The story of Justin's own rise to fame unfortunately began with the tearful breakup of his parents when he was a baby. Overwhelmed by the pressures of their teenage relationship, Justin's mother and father divorced when he was just ten months old. It was certainly a difficult time; one that Justin would not remember, but which would play a major role in his early years. After the divorce, Pattie reverted to her maiden name of Mallette and moved back home with her parents for a short time, while Justin's father returned to his hometown of Winnipeg.

'I didn't sing in public till I was twelve. My mom knew I could sing, though.'
– Justin Bieber

His mother would eventually win full custody of Justin. As a single woman, raising a son all by herself, life would certainly not be easy. 'Single mothers, an unheard of statistic, live below the poverty line,' said Pattie. 'I had no idea how I was going to get my next meal.'

Though Justin would rise years later to become one of the richest and most treasured teens in the world, he and his mother struggled early on, living in public housing in one of the poorest areas of Stratford. 'I worked two jobs to make ends meet,' Pattie said. 'But we had all the essentials.' Although life would bring its challenges from the start, mother and son were happy and felt lucky just to have each other. 'I had a roof above my head,' Justin said, 'and I basically had anything I wanted.'

Pattie Mallette grew up in Stratford as part of a troubled household. Her sister passed away in a car accident at the age of five, which led to a very difficult childhood and some unhappy teenage years for Pattie. In her early teens, she ran away from home. But by her late adolescence, she underwent a religious transformation and became a born-again Christian. A petite yet strong-willed woman, her ardent faith was central to Justin's upbringing as she struggled through multiple jobs to put food on the table. Perhaps it was Pattie's hard work and devotion that made Justin recognize how important his mother is in his life. 'I can't live without my mom,' he said.

The music gene runs deep in Justin's veins. His mother had musical aspirations of her own in her youth, and Justin was eager for the chance to follow in her footsteps. She graduated from Juliet School and North Western High School in Stratford in 1996. A fan of soulful tunes by Boyz II Men, she had performed in local stage productions as a girl. In her teens she worked extremely hard to get accepted onto a music program in Toronto. However, Justin's grandparents would not allow her to attend the school. Given that she never had the chance to pursue this dream, she later fully supported her son when the time came for him to begin his own music career. 'My mom when she was younger, she wanted to be an actress, and she got in a few local shows,' Justin said to Katie Couric of CBS. 'She wanted to go to this school in Toronto, which was two hours away, and my grandparents didn't let her. They didn't give her the chance. So my mom said [to me], "I want you to have this opportunity."'

Justin's father was also an avid musician. A skilled guitarist, Jeremy still teaches his son a few chords here and there when Justin is out on the road traveling. Even though he would move to Winnipeg and remarry, Justin's father loved his first son very much and did his best to remain a constant part of his world. Jeremy, nicknamed 'lordrauhl' in the online Spades card-game world, had recognized Justin's incredible musical gift early on and frequently touted his son as 'the most talented person I know' on his gaming profiles. Jeremy would later have two more children in his second marriage. Justin was blessed with a half-brother named Jaxon, and a little half-sister named Jazmyn, both of whom he still sees regularly.

However, without his father around all the time, life was difficult for young Justin. Given

A star and his guitar: Justin strums his stuff during a performance on The Today Show, *October 2009.*

his small physical stature and impoverished background, he was regularly teased and taunted about his second-hand clothes or scrappy size. Sometimes being the cutest kid in the playground doesn't protect you from the bullies, so Justin faced some challenges along the way. Although one of Pattie's friends would try his hardest to act as a father figure for her son, it simply wasn't the same without Justin's dad nearby to talk to about his problems or jam with on the guitar as a distraction. But Justin proved to be strong-willed at a young age. Although his father was far away in another part of the country, Justin had music, sports, school, and his friends to get him through the tough times. 'My hobbies – I play, like, ice hockey, basketball, golf. I scream and squeal on my guitar,' Justin beamed in an interview with a German reporter in May 2010. Plus, his mom made him the center of her world; she was always there to make sure he was happy and okay. 'I grew up below the poverty line; I didn't have as much as other people did,' Justin said. 'I think it made me stronger as a person, it built my character.'

'I wasn't poor. But I definitely did not have a lot of money.'
– Justin Bieber

For Justin, Stratford was just a regular small town where he and his friends could hang out and act like normal kids. But since Justin has achieved global stardom, Stratford has experienced a noticeable increase in tourism as avid fans flock to the city to learn more Bieber history. The local travel alliance even created the city's very own map to the stars, called *Bieber-iffic! Map to Stratford.* Highlighting a number of places where Justin and his best pals used to hang, the guide explores eighteen of Justin's favorite spots in the city. At the top of the list, of course, is the Avon Theater, best known as the spot where Justin played guitar during tourism season and earned roughly $150

to $200 a day busking on the steps for passersby. Given that Justin was a standout student, the map also includes all four of the schools that he attended.

His mom taught Justin the value of education at an early age. Justin attended elementary grades at a French immersion school (where he quickly picked up his second language), before going onto Avon Public School, Bedford Public School, and Downie Central Public School. Justin certainly worked hard in his classes, and frequently achieved grading reports worthy of being prominently displayed on the refrigerator. He worked his hardest for straight As, like a model student should. Before breaking into music, he hoped to one day attend university, get a great job and buy his mom all the things they never had. (Even at age sixteen, he still has a perfect 4.0 grade point average and says he wants to go to college.) However, Justin has also admitted to telling a pretty big fib about one of his tests back in grade school. Apparently, he changed a failing grade to a passing one so that his mother wouldn't find out that he'd flunked the test. 'A couple of years ago, I had an F grade on a test at school, but I turned it into a B with the teacher's pen!' Justin told *Top of the Pops* magazine. 'My mom had to sign that she'd seen it before I took it back, so she had no idea how bad it actually was!' Of course, Pattie didn't learn about this until recently and certainly wouldn't have approved of such naughty behavior. Had she found out, Justin would probably have been grounded for a period of time and forbidden from joining his friends at all his favorite hotspots.

'She wanted to go to this school in Toronto, which was two hours away, and my grandparents didn't let her. They didn't give her the chance. So my mum said [to me], "I want you to have this opportunity."'
– Justin Bieber

When he wasn't in school, Justin and his friends worked on their skateboarding tricks at the skate park east of Downie Street. But Pattie definitely kept an eye on who Justin hung around with after school, making sure that he was in good company. 'My mom is strict. She sets boundaries. She's very concerned about who I'm going out with and who's an influence on my life.' Of course, Pattie surely approved of Justin's best friend Ryan Butler, who he met when he was just six years old, and his other partners-in-crime, Christian Beadles and Chaz Somers. When they were done shredding along the skate park during weekends, Justin and his best friends also liked to work up an appetite and sharpen their pool skills at a local pub called the Pour House just a few blocks down the street.

Being that he is of French, German, and Ukrainian descent, Justin was no stranger to a number of different cuisines. Although he was a small kid, he had a big appetite. When Justin wanted a breakfast fit for a king, he and his friends would go to a restaurant called Features on Ontario Street. But no matter how big his appetite grew over the years, it is doubtful that he would have been able to polish off the restaurant's most famous dish, the Paul Bunyan – an enormous spread of eggs, bacon, French toast, pancakes, and breakfast potatoes. Dinner-wise, Justin liked to stick to his favorite dish, spaghetti. According to Justin, no place was better for spaghetti than Madelyn's Diner, his mom's favorite restaurant. Sure, he and his friends would go there for breakfast, as it was a preferred spot for Northwestern students – but some quiet time with his mother and a big plate of pasta were his rewards after long days of school and sports.

Above: Justin and his mentor Usher Raymond perform together onstage at Madison Square Garden, December 2009.
Below: Industry player Justin pictured with (left to right) Doug Morris, chairman of UMG; L.A. Reid, chairman of Island Def Jam; and 'Umbrella' singer Rihanna, New York, December 2009.

It would be spaghetti that later got him into trouble on his first real date. King's Buffet on Ontario Street was the location of Justin's first attempt at winning a girl's heart through her stomach. Given that he liked spaghetti so much, a pasta dinner seemed like the perfect way for him and his new girl to get to know each other. Unfortunately, Justin's dining etiquette was hardly smooth. Perhaps nerves got the better of him, as he spilled spaghetti and meatballs all over himself in front of the young lady. His mess didn't earn him a second date.

It may seem hard to believe now, with millions of girls out there all clamoring to be the Bieb's 'Favorite Girl,' but back in those days a single Justin was actually forced to dine by himself from time to time. He would frequently grab a bite from the Subway sandwich shop on Huron Street after school or one of his sports games. Justin, a star athlete who played hockey, basketball and soccer, typically worked up an appetite playing sports for several of Stratford's youth travel teams, including the city's travel soccer team – the Stratford Strikers – at the Cooper Standard Soccer Fields and the travel hockey team at the William Allman Memorial Arena.

'She's a really strong woman. She's been there since day one, just wanting me to be the best person I can be. She doesn't care about the money, the fame; she just wants to be my mom.'
– Justin Bieber

The most important pastime for young Justin, however, was music. Given his mother's fondness for singing, she quickly realized that Justin was musically inclined from a young age. 'I was always singing around the house, it was just something I loved to do. I always played a lot of different instruments. I kind of grew up around music my whole life,' he told watchmojo.com. He also had a habit of banging on pots and pans and any other appliance in the house that would make a sound. 'I was basically banging on everything I could get my hands on,' Justin said. Seeking to accommodate her son's newfound pleasure in creating a racket, Pattie purchased him a small drum set when he was just four years old. 'I started the drums really early. I was, like, two years old. My mom was crazy enough to buy me a drum kit when I was four.' As he grew up, he would eventually adapt his skills to other instruments after seeing people play them at his church, where Justin was a member of the choir. Keeping an ear to the lively tunes of Stevie Wonder and Michael Jackson, the fresh-faced Justin started to play the piano at seven, taught himself the guitar at nine and put his lips to the trumpet at age thirteen. It was simply incredible that a young kid with no formal training in any of these instruments could just pick one of them up and learn how to play. But learning four was an astonishing accomplishment. 'I guess you can say I've been blessed with talent,' Justin said.

Justin's early days in Stratford were certainly tough given that his father was absent and his mom struggled to support their family. But Justin constantly looks back on that time with a smile, thankful that his mom did so much to make his childhood happy and healthy. Even when he reflects and realizes that he didn't have much, he always returns to the fact that his mom was loving and giving enough to offer her child the loudest instrument that she could find for him to bang in their little apartment. 'What mom in her right mind would buy a four-year-old a drum kit?' Justin laughed. The answer was simple: a mother who would soon allow her talented son to follow his dreams in music.

The point: A purple-clad Justin performs during the Arthur Ashe Kids' Day at the US Tennis Open, New York, August 2009.

Worldwide Wonder

'My friends and family that couldn't be there [asked], "You sing?" So I said, "Yeah, I sing, a little bit."'

– Justin Bieber

By the tender age of twelve, the Stratford-based sweetheart had already taught himself four different instruments. But who would have guessed – besides his protective mom Pattie – that behind his gentle smile, a soulful voice was just waiting to be discovered? As with his instruments, Justin didn't have any vocal training. 'I wasn't taking it too seriously at the time, I would just sing around the house,' Justin said. Single mom Pattie simply couldn't afford to send Justin to music lessons; if he wanted a shot at fame, he would have to train himself once again. What he lacked in professional tutoring, he made up for with a real passion for music and a natural voice that could soar to hit the highest, most difficult notes.

Certainly, he'd performed in the church choir, but with so many different talents, Justin couldn't wait to step into the spotlight for his big solo. At an age when most kids would be intimidated to sing in front of a large audience, Justin proved that he could stay cool under pressure. Quietly confident in his own ability, Justin soon entered a local singing contest at the Kiwanis Community Centre, called Stratford Idol – inspired by the immensely popular *American Idol* series. 'I was eleven or twelve. Basically what got me started, I was in a singing competition,' Justin told news anchor Katie Couric of CBS. 'It was really kind of a talent show, because you win, but you don't really win anything. It was just kind of [for fun].'

While many singers in the contest had picked their favorite artists and imitated their songs note for note, for Justin this simply wouldn't do. Hungry for a challenge, he took to the stage with a performance that would set him apart from the pack. While he stuck to established favorites, he also showed judges that he could employ his unique style within each rendition. Justin sang four songs: Aretha Franklin's girl-power anthem 'Respect,' Matchbox 20's '3 A.M.,' Alicia Keys' 'Fallin',' and finally 'So Sick' by one of his favorite artists, Ne-Yo. His set list was certainly a

Geek chic: Justin sports a pair of oversized spectacles as he enters
The Today Show's *studios, New York, October 2009.*

challenge, but the gamble would surely pay off if he performed well. Justin knew that he couldn't succeed if he didn't take chances in the competition, and in life.

So how did Justin perform in Stratford Idol? Surprising even himself, he finished in second place against a pool of singers who had vocal training and significant singing experience. 'The other people in the competition had been taking singing lessons and had vocal coaches,' Justin said in an interview with jb-source.org. Having practiced around the apartment for years, Justin had only entered the contest for his own enjoyment. 'I just did it for fun,' he told neonlimelight.com. 'I wasn't trying to be famous or anything.'

Justin shined, setting himself apart from his competitors. A natural-born showman, he turned his brown cap around and couldn't stop his feet moving to the catchy backing track for '3 A.M.' and even treated the audience to an improvisational solo on the air saxophone midway through his version of 'Respect' – dropping his microphone in the process. Instantly charmed by his charismatic moves, the audience were soon dancing along. Even back then, baby-faced Justin had a voice as smooth as silk. No one in the crowd would have guessed he'd been singing for just three years and gained much of his vocal training in the shower. One listen was all it took to realize that this talented kid had a bright future ahead of him. In fact, the only person not to know this was Justin himself, despite finishing in second place.

'I looked up to Michael Jackson and Stevie Wonder and Boyz II Men. But I never tried to sound like anybody.'
– Justin Bieber

Still, Justin wasn't entirely satisfied with his success in the competition. Pattie had been there to cheer him on, but what of the other close friends and family members who'd missed it? Family-oriented Justin wanted to share the experience with everyone in his life, and so Pattie, having become web savvy in recent years, posted her recording on YouTube – a website designed for sharing videos with others. For Justin, it was the ideal solution. 'My family and friends [. . .] they wanted to be there but they couldn't, so I put videos of the competition on YouTube [. . .] just for them.'

Pretty soon it wasn't just his family who were paying attention to the angel-voiced teen. Justin's ability to capture the raw emotion behind the mature, meaningful songs that he'd chosen was something truly unique – and fans everywhere were quickly taking notice, forwarding his video to friends. One person told two people and those two people told ten. Justin couldn't believe how popular he'd become; people all over the world were tuning in to listen to him and he wasn't even a professional singer. 'It was crazy because, I looked and I got 100 views, and I don't have 100 family members,' Justin said. 'That was a lot at the time. And then I got 200 views and it just kept coming up. So I said, "Let's just keep putting up videos and see what happens."' He and his mother had no idea that this sudden attention was just the tip of the iceberg – the beginning of something special. 'Being famous was never in my mind,' Justin smiled shyly. 'Like, Stratford, Ontario . . . a little town of 30,000 in the middle of nowhere? It was something I didn't think was possible. I owe everything to my fans and YouTube.'

Another benefit of using YouTube became instantly apparent – listeners were able to provide feedback, telling him just how much they loved his songs. They could also tell him that they wanted to hear more. Lots more. Justin soon began to record a string of home performances, deep emotional versions of his favorite songs. Clutching one hand over his heart while the other motioned to his audience, he put his own spin on chart-topping songs by hit artists like Usher, Justin Timberlake, Ne-Yo and Stevie Wonder. Despite the common misconception that he created hundreds of videos, Justin only actually posted about ten short performances – all of which quickly went viral, burning up the YouTube ratings and receiving hits from all around the

Dream lover: Justin brings the romance for a special Valentine's Day concert at the Hollywood Palladium, February 2010.

globe. No one was more surprised than Justin himself. 'I gave [my friends and family] the link and they went and watched it. Just a bunch of people started watching it, so [it] started getting more hits and more hits,' he said. Neither Pattie nor Justin could believe it. But, looking back, it's easy to see how he created such a stir. With his glossy locks and sweet smile, Justin has the talent to match his adorable good looks.

With millions of people all over the world signing on for their daily dose of Justin's music, you'd be forgiven for thinking that this was all part of some master plan to jumpstart his career. But that just isn't Justin's style. With this young star, what you see is what you get. And Justin was just doing what he loved – entertaining his friends and family. 'People always say, "Did you try to get famous off YouTube?" I'm like, "Not at all." I was just doing it for fun.' And, besides, he was also doing this in secret. 'I didn't tell my friends,' Justin told *Billboard*, 'because they didn't really know that I could sing. They knew me for playing sports. I just wanted to be a regular kid, and I knew that they wouldn't treat me the same way if I told them.' Justin was now a young man with separate identities. At school, he was a popular athlete who liked the attention of girls and enjoyed hanging out with his friends at the hockey rink. In the evening hours, he was kidrauhl, the internet sensation performing for his growing worldwide YouTube audience.

'I really just did it for friends and family. Then other people started watching it.'
– Justin Bieber

This much was for sure: people were craving more of Justin's music and so, in addition to performing more and more songs online, he decided it was time to take his act to the streets – literally. At the age of thirteen, he spent an entire summer on the steps of Stratford's Avon Theater, strumming his acoustic guitar and belting out versions of his own favorite ballads – with a few he'd penned himself thrown in for good measure. 'I would play outside, and I would put out my guitar case, and people would, like, throw any change, and stuff,' Justin explained to *MTV News*. 'And I made 3,000 dollars and I took my mom on a vacation to Florida. Yeah, it was pretty awesome.' Although he initially said that he wanted to busk in order to make some money so that he could go golfing with his friends, he later decided to treat his mother as thanks for all of her love and support over the years. 'He took us on our first vacation ever,' a proud Pattie revealed. 'We went to Disneyland.' Videos of his theater-step performances also began to appear online, recorded by local fans and tourists who had been stopped in their tracks by the sound of Justin's voice. Justin Bieber was now an online sensation and local fixture in Stratford. Fans all over the world were smitten – and it was only a matter of time before someone in the music industry caught on to the craze for the super-cute young singer.

Pretty soon, he received an email from Rapid Discovery Media in Toronto offering to help him build on his popularity. A social networking and audio-visual marketing company that helps artists promote their work online, Rapid Discovery Media had been extremely impressed by Justin's talent and enthusiasm. Company bosses were convinced that Justin could reach even more fans via popular social-networking sites like MySpace. Intrigued by the limitless possibilities, Justin and Pattie agreed. Rapid Discovery Media helped Justin to tweak his videos, adding professional polish to the sound and visuals. They also revamped his 'kidrauhl' channel on YouTube (making Justin's performances more accessible) and even created biography and blog sections on his MySpace page. With so many fans all around the world, the company really helped Justin reach his audience and, more importantly, showed the talented teen that a future in the music business was well within his reach, if he could only go the distance. With the company's help, Justin added a few more videos – performances of Justin Timberlake and Michael Jackson songs – and promoted his renditions on a slew of different websites. Word immediately spread of his new recordings and people quickly tuned into his YouTube channel. By the end of the year, he would have more than one million views of every one of his songs. Ultimately, he would generate an incredible ten million views of his songs and videos of him playing sports, simply via word of mouth as fans eagerly traded the links in emails, text messages, blogs, and Twitter posts. In February 2008, Justin recorded one of his most memorable amateur performances of Chris Brown's hit song 'With You.' His little YouTube channel had generated so much traffic and buzz that even the original performer of the song got to see Justin's version. Within days, Brown called Justin to praise his performance. Certainly, Brown knew that people all over the world were singing his songs, but he never would have expected that someone like Justin – an ordinary kid from Ontario – could come along and wow him. Justin was naturally thrilled that one of his favorite singers liked his version so much. But that wasn't enough for him. If Justin wanted to go from Stratford to the major labels, he'd need music executives to take notice and call him up. It just so happened that in Atlanta, one prominent music mogul was surfing the web, scouring social-networking sites for new potential talent. What happened next was reportedly just an accident, as the Atlanta-based Scooter Braun clicked on one of Justin's videos in a slip that would change Justin's future forever.

> **'People always say, "Did you try to get famous off YouTube?" I'm like, "Not at all." I was just doing it for fun.'**
> **– Justin Bieber**

Justin gets into the Christmas spirit while performing at Madison Square Garden for Z100's Jingle Ball, December 2009.

3

Clash of the Heartthrobs

'Justin Bieber – from the moment that I met him, I recognized that he was poised to be successful.'

– Usher Raymond

With more than ten million views on YouTube by mid-2008 and thousands of fans visiting his MySpace page, Justin Bieber had become a genuine online phenomenon, one capable of generating a passionate following despite his relative anonymity. The possibilities and his talent were limitless, but millions of views on social-media sites did not guarantee mainstream success or a record contract. Earlier in the past decade, the music industry had shunned performers who used websites to promote their talent. Certainly, great musicians were out there waiting to be discovered, but finding them proved to be a major challenge for anyone in the music business. For every video uploaded by the immensely talented Justin Bieber, there were thousands and thousands of off-key postings by amateur musicians billing themselves as the next Justin Timberlake or Kelly Clarkson. Given the time and patience needed to recruit artists in the online world, the internet was initially viewed by many talent scouts as a waste of both.

But the music industry has changed in recent years. Fans now prefer iTunes and iPods to compact discs and portable CD players. They regularly go online for news about their favorite artists in addition to picking up magazines and newspapers. For artists of the MySpace generation, there are other ways of getting their music heard than scoring a record deal. In response to changing trends, industry executives began to understand the importance of music downloads and social networking. MySpace had quickly become a go-to resource for artists and bands looking to promote and sell their music to the world; YouTube too had risen to prominence as the most dynamic music- and video-sharing site, providing easy access to anyone interested in watching more original, user-generated material.

In Atlanta, music manager Scooter Braun was way ahead of the curve and on the lookout for the next breakout star on the web. Having originally started as a party and musician promoter

Whatever the leather: Justin is all smiles as he signs copies of
My World at a branch of HMV in London, January 2010.

while a student at Emory University, Braun had quickly established himself as one of music's most knowledgeable recruiters, with a keen eye for the 'next big thing.' At just nineteen, Braun had already earned the respect of producer Jermaine Dupri, best known for his work on Usher's album *Confessions* and Mariah Carey's *The Emancipation of Mimi*. Dupri offered Braun a job with his label So So Def Records as the executive director of marketing and Braun naturally accepted.

Braun had become so popular by the age of twenty-three that his decision to quit as marketing director of So So Def Records sent shockwaves through the R&B industry. In fact the ambitious young mogul was founding his own company, Scooter Braun Projects. Named by *Billboard* as one of the top thirty-under-thirty power players of 2009, the ambitious entrepreneur set an aggressive agenda for himself as a potential manager of rising talent. While attending a basketball game with his friend Chaka Zulu, manager of Ludacris, he laid out three critical short-term goals for his company. In the wake of the success of rapper Marshall Mathers, also known as Eminem, Braun was in search of the next breakthrough Caucasian rap star, one with a strong underground presence. Within two weeks of stating this objective, he signed MC Asher Roth, a cheery white rapper best known his constant smile and the hit university anthem 'I Love College.' Braun's next goal (although whether he ever accomplished this is still unclear) was to find an all-conquering girl group, inspired by the global success of the Spice Girls in the 1990s. Braun's third goal was the most ambitious yet. He sought to find the next teenage singer who 'could do it like Michael Jackson.' According to Billboard.com, Scooter Braun was in search of the musical Holy Grail, and embarked upon a national hunt for a versatile young star who could 'sing songs that adults would appreciate and be reminded of the innocence they once felt about love.' Forget the haystack; Braun's mission was to find the needle buried somewhere underneath. Was it possible that Justin Bieber could be that star?

> 'My mom was basically like, "Justin, I don't think this is going to happen, it's not going to work, we don't have a lawyer, we don't have money for a lawyer, and we're not going to just sign something that we don't know what it says."'
> – Justin Bieber

That depended on a number of different factors, above all the permission of his mother. At the same time, Pattie Mallette was praying that her son would become the next famous singer on the Christian music circuit, a 'modern Prophet Samuel' who could spread the word of God and recruit people to join their Church (something that early on, Justin's MySpace profile listed as one of his foremost ambitions). Justin had received a number of calls from parties interested in recruiting the amateur singer to sign a contract or perform on television. But Pattie kept finding excuses to turn down these proposals, delaying Justin's progress until her son received an offer that met with her moral expectations. According to Justin, his mother repeatedly told him, 'Sorry Justin, we don't have a lawyer.' She didn't want to see him exploited by the first industry shark who came along, and hoped her gifted young son would understand. A controversial American talk-show host was the first to reach out to the young star, but the offer was quickly shot down by Ms Mallette. 'Well first, basically, I got this email from Maury Povich,' Justin told Katie Couric. 'He wanted me on this show to do this competition. And my mom was like, "No." [My mother is] a single mom, so she was really skeptical of the music business. She had no clue. We didn't have a lawyer. We didn't want to sign anything. So we said "no" to Maury, no disrespect [to him].'

At the same time that the talk-show circuit was attempting to recruit Justin, Scooter Braun was hard at work on his third goal of locating that singer with the same glowing potential as a young Michael Jackson. He'd spent hours and hours scouring YouTube, but somehow missed the amazing talent just waiting to be discovered in Stratford. That would quickly change when his search led him to a twenty-year-old singer on YouTube who was performing his own variation of Aretha Franklin's immortal hit 'Respect.' Impressed by this singer's range and talent, Braun wanted to see the other songs that had been posted on the musician's channel. But then a funny thing happened. Someone had linked a video of Justin to that performer's page. Thinking that Justin's video was another version by the same twenty-year-old singer, Braun unwittingly clicked on the link. 'I was consulting for an act that Akon had in a production deal and looking at his YouTube videos,' Braun said. 'The kid was singing Aretha Franklin's "Respect." I clicked on it thinking it was the same kid and realized that the twenty-year-old I was watching was now twelve.'

Braun was instantly stunned by the natural talent he'd discovered with a random click of his computer mouse. 'It was Justin in his first ever singing competition at twelve years old. I was blown away that a little kid had a range like that.' He immediately viewed all of the videos posted by 'kidrauhl.' Convinced that he had found his Michael Jackson-in-the-making, Braun started a full-scale detective

Mom's the word: Justin and his mother Pattie dressed to impress at the glamorous Fifty-Second Annual Grammy Awards, Los Angeles, January 2010.

effort to track down the young Canadian that would have impressed the greatest investigators. The music manager reached out to every single person he could find who might know Justin's whereabouts. 'He stalked us a little bit,' Justin said with a laugh. Braun called every school in Stratford, searched photo archives of the theater where Justin had made his vacation money, and called Justin's relatives and school-board members. He pleaded with anyone who knew Justin to contact Ms Mallette and beg her to let him discuss her son's amazing talents. 'He was very, very persistent,' Justin said. 'He even called my great aunt and my school board.'

'When he was five, he'd hear something on the radio and go to the keyboard and figure it out.' – Pattie Mallette

Determined not to let Justin's unique talent slip through his fingers, Braun wouldn't give up. He was convinced that Justin Bieber was the real deal, the next big thing. 'My gut was going crazy,' Braun said. 'So I tracked him down. 'At the time, Ms Mallette thought that Braun was just another music marketer seeking to exploit her son's talent, but the more they talked, the more she began to trust his future manager's motivations. Self-described as 'very protective' and still holding onto the dream that Justin would become a Christian singing sensation, she prayed again for guidance. 'I prayed, "God, you don't want this [. . .] kid to be Justin's man, do you?"' Braun continued to make his sales pitch. Where once Ms Mallette considered telling Braun to leave her and Justin alone, she quickly found that he offered the answers she sought. '[Scooter Braun] was like, "I really see a lot in your son, I think I can help you guys,"' Justin said. Braun even helped address Pattie's largest concern about her son's potential career. 'He knew some lawyers that we could talk to.' Pleading that he believed Justin had the potential to become an international megastar with the right guidance, Braun offered to fly both Justin and his mother to Atlanta for a formal face-to-face meeting.

Although she had not envisioned her son as a mainstream pop sensation, she turned to her Church elders, who encouraged her to allow Justin to follow this dream. Pretty soon, Justin signed a management deal with Braun, and mother and son boarded that jet to Atlanta. 'That was the first time either of them had been on a plane,' Braun said. 'They weren't a wealthy family . . . his mom worked different jobs and their grandparents kind of helped out, so they got by.'

When Justin and Pattie arrived in Atlanta, Scooter drove them around town and scheduled a session at a recording studio, where Justin could create a few sample tracks. Now that Braun had finally won her over, Pattie allowed him to start searching for a major label to sign her son. But, much as his mother's sudden approval of a career in pop may have shocked him, it certainly wouldn't be the biggest surprise of Justin's day. Later that afternoon, on the way to a supermarket, Justin had his first encounter with music megastar Usher Raymond IV, although he'd walk away disappointed by the experience. 'Usher happens to roll up [to the studio] in his Range Rover, so I was like, "Man, that's Usher."' An excited Justin hustled up to the five-time Grammy Award-winner and panted, 'Hey Usher, I love your songs, do you want me to sing you one?' Thinking Justin was just another fan trying to impress him, Usher naturally dismissed the teen, saying, 'That's okay little buddy. It's cold out. Why don't you just come inside?' Usher had given Justin the cold shoulder. But it was just a matter of time before the world-famous recording artist would realize that he had made a mistake in underestimating the ambitious young talent from Ontario.

'I was really impressed with how young he was and how he was holding the crowd and with his guitar and, you know, he was raw talent.'
– Scooter Braun

Over the next few weeks, Scooter was pushing Justin's YouTube videos to the biggest producers in music, comparing him to the King of Pop, Michael Jackson. However, Braun was finding that without the backing of Disney or a big-name television show to showcase his client's talent, these music moguls didn't see Justin as a marketable star. 'Everyone had told me, "You don't have a Nickelodeon or Disney show. You can't break Justin." I wanted him to be the next Michael Jackson,' Braun said. 'And literally everyone said "no." But his talent was undeniable, and his success is a testament to his true ability.' Eventually interest would build in signing the Canadian heartthrob. One of the first music executives to express serious interest was Charlie Walk, then president of Epic. Sony Music had recently partnered with Nickelodeon to jointly produce several rocking new shows and albums for fans hungry for fresh talent. Within a few days of seeing Justin's YouTube videos, Walk contacted Nickelodeon's senior vice president of music marketing and talent, Doug Cohn, about creating a show for Justin. But it wasn't meant to be. Epic passed on him because there was no show available at the time. But Justin has demonstrated a 'never give up' attitude, as revealed in numerous tweets to his followers – and he and Braun were definitely not about to quit after coming so far.

Of course they were both frustrated by the failure to ink a deal with Epic, but Braun quickly called his old friend Justin Timberlake, perhaps the only star around today who can touch Michael Jackson in terms of his slick dance routines, irresistible pop tunes and undeniable selling power. 'I wanted to bring in another artist to put his stamp on Justin,' Braun said. '[Justin] Timberlake just signed Esmée Denters to Tennman Records, Timberlake's label, so I thought he might understand the space. I went to him, and he was 100 percent in.' Timberlake was instantly impressed by the young teen's range and skills and set up a meeting with Justin, his mother and Braun in Los Angeles.

For the moment, it seemed that Justin was on his way to creating an album with Tennman, a joint venture between Justin Timberlake and Interscope Records. But a few weeks later, Braun sat down with Usher and a computer and showed him Justin's YouTube videos. Awestruck by what he saw, Usher immediately scheduled a meeting of his own. But at the time he first saw the videos, Usher didn't realize that Justin was the same young kid that he'd dismissed in the parking lot of the studio weeks

My hero: Is it a bird? No, it's Justin on a visit to Six Flags Magic Mountain, May 2010.

prior. 'I said, "You've met him already,"' Braun laughed. 'Usher was like, "I thought he was your cousin or something."' Now concerned about his error, a red-faced Usher hustled to recruit Justin just one day after Braun and his client had their final meeting with Timberlake in Los Angeles. '[Usher] actually watched my videos and was like, "Man, I should have let this kid sing,"' Justin Bieber said. 'And he flew me back to Atlanta. I got to sing for him, and then a week later, I had a meeting with Justin Timberlake. They both kind of wanted me.'

Usher flew Justin and his mother back to Atlanta for a private audition. Videos of Justin's try-out reveal a confident young showman with a cheeky smile, his hat swiveled backwards and his Toronto Maple Leafs jersey prominently on display. Hitting the high notes with a hand over his heart, Justin pauses in the middle of one of Usher's signature songs, 'U Got It Bad,' to ask the Grammy-winner, 'Are you gonna sing with me or what?' A leather-jacket-clad Usher

'Back in Canada I told everybody, "Yeah, I met Usher," and they were like, "Yeah, right."'
– Justin Bieber

remains on the edge of his seat, looking on in awe, his shoulders hunched forward as he hangs on every perfect note. 'He sang my own song better than me,' Usher later told talk-show host Ellen DeGeneres. A bidding war quickly formed between Timberlake and Usher. 'I was twelve or thirteen at the time,' Justin said about the sudden attention from two of the biggest names in music. 'My head was definitely spinning. It was kind of a surreal moment.'

*Left: Justin brings the curtain down on one of the best years of his life with a sensational performance on Dick Clark's New Year's Rockin' Eve, Las Vegas, December 2009. **Right:** Two of a kind: Justin and Usher attend KIIS FM's Wango Tango, Los Angeles, May 2010.*

Usher desperately wanted to sign Bieber, but he knew that Justin Timberlake had made an offer and had his own record label in Tennman. But where Timberlake had the resources, Usher was confident that he had the determination to make Justin a global star. 'He just had a star quality that just comes once in a lifetime,' Usher said. 'But more than anything it was the fact that he would develop to be such an incredible talent. The fact that he can play keys, he can play guitar, he can play drums, and he taught himself, that just showed just how much determination he had as a musician. To be self-taught and to want to emulate the artists that he would sing their songs.' Willing to go to any lengths to seal the deal, Usher even offered to take Justin shopping. 'It turned out Usher's deal was way better,' Justin said simply. 'He had L.A. Reid backing him and Scooter had a lot of really good connections in Atlanta.' With the backing of producing legend L.A. Reid, Usher knew that he had the ability to make Justin a global phenomenon.

'I couldn't believe they were fighting over me. It's just crazy!'
– Justin Bieber

Like everyone who had met the teen wonder, Reid, who had signed Usher at the age of fourteen, was immediately impressed by Justin. 'I thought he was an amazing kid, charming with loads of personality,' said Reid. Most important in the deal with Reid was that Justin's lack of a television platform – something that had rattled bosses at Tennman – was of no concern to anyone. 'I've never had the benefit of an *American Idol*,' Reid said. 'Maybe it's dated, but we launch artists in the traditional sense. Oftentimes, while these kids may be very talented, we think of them as TV stars first, and the music is secondary. Justin is music first.'

After receiving competitive offers from both sides, Braun steered Justin toward Usher's camp as both men shared the belief that this teen was destined for stardom. 'Usher didn't have a label yet, so he wanted to be my partner,' Braun said. 'Timberlake wanted to be my partner, but the people running his label weren't as keen on it. Usher understood the role I wanted him to play.' In October of 2008, Justin Bieber officially signed a joint contract with partners Usher and Scooter Braun's new label RBMG and Island Records. Although Usher had given Braun the freedom to manage and craft Justin, he considered it a small price to pay for the once-in-a-lifetime talent that his friend had discovered online. '[Justin Bieber] was an amazing talent and find,' Usher said. 'Given my experience, I knew exactly what it would take for him to become an incredible artist.'

'He just had a star quality that comes once in a lifetime, but more than anything it was the fact that he would develop to be such an incredible talent. The fact that he can play keys, he can play guitar, he can play drums and he taught himself, that showed just how much determination he had as a musician. To be self-taught and to want to emulate the artists that he would sing their songs.'
– Usher Raymond

It was not just Usher's experience in the music business that convinced him he was exactly the right person to promote the handsome young teen. The similarities in the life stories of Usher Raymond and Justin Bieber are almost uncanny. Usher began his singing career in Atlanta at the age of nine in his mother's church choir; Justin's mother was a very devout woman who was incredibly protective of her son and encouraged him to join the church choir at an early age. Both musicians got their jump start in amateur singing competitions; Justin in the Stratford Idol contest and Usher on the very prestigious TV show *Star Search*. Usher was signed at the age of fourteen by L.A. Reid; while Justin was ushered into L.A. Reid's office at the same age to ink a deal. (According to Braun, Reid frequently says that he finds it ironic that 'Justin was the same exact age as Usher when he was signed.') Both Justin and Usher are incredibly close to their mothers, with whom both grew up in single-parent households. Usher's father left his family when he was one year old, while Justin's parents split when he was only ten months old.

Perhaps the most important similarity between the superstar and the star-in-the-making was that both had been blessed with immense musical talent and personal drive in their early years and seemed to have fame sewn into their destinies. 'There was an ultimate star quality about him,' Usher said. 'I saw that he wanted it. It was the same fire I had. He was so talented, even more than I was at [that age]. From the moment that I met him, I recognized that he was poised to be successful.' Justin would be expected to work quickly on his debut album. A few weeks later, Pattie Mallette and Justin Bieber moved to Atlanta to begin this dream-come-true career. With L.A. Reid and Usher now backing him, it was just a matter of time before Justin would shoot to the top of the charts and into the hearts of millions. 'I think it's amazing that I was able to come off the internet and just break into the mainstream and be an artist all around the world,' Justin said. 'It's pretty incredible.'

Justin's World

'He's a young kid who sings with a lot more soul than he should.'

– Scooter Braun

It wouldn't take long for everyone in the studio to come into contact with Justin's cheeky sense of humor. Since the day that Justin signed a contract with Island Def Jam, Biebs has frequently teased his friend and mentor Usher about their awkward first encounter in the parking lot, when the chipper young star was not allowed to 'audition' for his idol. But even though Justin would gain a reputation for his verbal digs, the bigwigs at the production company recognized his maturity and dedication when the time came to record his first album. 'He jokes and kids and teases, but when it's time for business, he's pretty much business,' said Chris Hicks, an Island Def Jam executive.

Usher and Island Def Jam were lucky that Justin didn't slip through their fingers. Thousands of fans from around the world knew about Justin's videos and talent and would have given anything to witness their own personal one-on-one performance. But Usher had dismissed his future protégé without a second's thought. Still, Justin recognizes that even if Usher had immediately been taken by his bubbly personality, it was really his mother who would make the ultimate decision as to whether or not he would have the chance to work with the legendary star. Luckily for everyone, Pattie wanted Justin to have that opportunity.

Much to his own surprise, Justin now had his first recording contract. 'I didn't really have plans to get a record deal or anything,' he told *MTV News*. 'I was just . . . it's kind of like luck, but when it happened I immediately knew that this was what I was born to do.' Now that he and his mom had moved to Atlanta, it was time to go to work. Justin's only previous recording experience had been for a charity song in Stratford, so questions about the process lingered. Would the fact that he had no formal vocal training hurt his performances? What sort of songs would he sing? And who would write his catchy pop tunes?

*Justin's much-imitated haircut takes center stage at Nickelodeon's
Twenty-Third Annual Kids' Choice Awards, Los Angeles, March 2010.*

All of his YouTube videos had been covers of his favorite songs. But now he was going to be working on new songs, quite a challenge for a young man barely in high school or tall enough to see over the kitchen counter. The biggest test that lay ahead was the need for Justin to create his own unique sound and image, or else people might think that he was simply copying other singers. Luckily, Justin has some of the best people in the business backing him up. His new musical team included Braun, Reid, and Ryan Good, one of Usher's former assistants, who was handpicked to be Justin's road manager and 'swagger coach.' As swagger coach, Good was in charge of sharpening Justin's dance moves, his on- and offstage attitude, and his signature wardrobe. Now Justin had someone other than his mom picking out his clothes in the morning, and looked sharper than ever when he went out in public.

But in the music business, it's not just the clothes that make the man. If Justin was going to become the next Michael Jackson, he'd have to devote his free hours – previously dedicated to skateboarding – to private singing lessons. Constantly looking for ways to improve himself, Justin accepted the record company's offer of professional tuition. And in his search for the right team to write signature tunes for his star-in-the-making, Braun recruited an army of lyrical talent, booking studio time with some of the top R&B and pop producers and songwriters in the business, including Terius 'The-Dream' Nash, Bryan-Michael Cox, Tricky Stewart, and Johntá Austin.

'I think that the internet is something that keeps your fans involved in the project. It's a new day and age. I think a lot of older artists didn't have the chance to use the internet and Facebook. It's a great way to bring your fans in.'
– Justin Bieber

A heavily promoted album and worldwide tour would have been the normal first steps for the Def Jam marketing team. However, Scooter Braun had a better idea. He decided to build on Justin's online success. Rather than booking time in the studio and recording an album right away, Braun and his team continued to create grainy YouTube videos of Justin singing in order to generate even more online buzz about the boy wonder. 'I wanted to build him up more on YouTube first,' Braun said. 'We supplied more content. I said, "Justin, sing like there's no one in the room. But let's not use expensive cameras." We'll give it to kids, let them do the work, so that they feel like it's theirs.'

The increased exposure on YouTube naturally accomplished two very important goals: first, it built on the cult-like following that Justin had already generated. Second, and more importantly, it would place Justin's career in the hands of his biggest fans. After all, it was them who had made him an international phenomenon, so why not give the 'Beliebers' more of what they wanted? Given that he was the number one online musician in Canada, Justin had time to slowly transition from online amateur singer and dancer to the global teen-pop icon of today.

Justin and the team were on their way to the recording studio. 'It was my first time ever being in the studio,' Justin said excitedly. 'I think my emotion has always been there, but I know what to do better now, and my voice has developed.' With the help of his team, Justin churned out eight catchy tunes for his LP. But if you're a fifteen-year-old newcomer, what do you call your first album? Justin would have to sit down and really think about a catchy, meaningful title. Should he have the title reflect his old life in Stratford or his new life in Atlanta? Should it be something about young love and the girls who had chased him? Or should he try to find a title that really captured everything about who he was? Luckily Justin had some inspiration from one of the songs that he and his team had already recorded.

Left: *Peace, man: Justin arrives at the Ed Sullivan Theater to film* The Late Show with David Letterman, *March 2010.*
Right: *Justin and infamous gossip blogger Perez Hilton, Los Angeles, March 2010.*

Justin decided that his first album should be called *My World*. 'I had the concept because we did this song called "My World," which wasn't on the album *My World*, weirdly enough. I was like, that should be the title of my album. It's just everything that is in my world. You know, girls, and school, and my parents split up when I was really little, but I still have a good relationship with both my mom and dad, but they split up when I was young.'

With *My World* complete, Justin's manager took the eight songs to L.A. Reid in February 2009 and played them for the producing legend. '[Reid] was like, "We've got singles. We're ready,"' Braun said. The first step in promoting Justin's new album was to have the company release one, two, or several singles to help generate buzz about the upcoming album. But which song should be released before the rest of the album? It was a tricky question for the producers to answer. The

> 'The album was just a blast and I think that having so much fun was reflected in the album. I think people saw that.'
> – Justin Bieber

track had to be the perfect tune to give all Justin's potential fans a taste of his flawlessly pitched voice. The pressure was on Justin and the rest of the team to make the right decision. Rolling the dice, they selected his now-immortal hit 'One Time.'

As expected, Justin didn't write the signature song. The tune was penned by Tricky Stewart and Terius 'The-Dream' Nash. Both men had years of experience writing some of the most popular R&B tunes of the decade, including Rihanna's 'Umbrella' and the global smash girl-anthem 'Single Ladies (Put a Ring On It)' by Beyoncé. Sure, writing for a fourteen-year-old would be one of the biggest challenges of their career, but both Stewart and Nash knew that with Justin's talent and their experience, they had all the makings of a major hit.

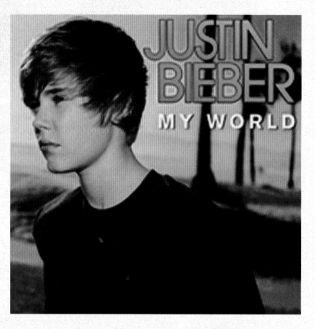

The catchy tune – like most of the other songs on Justin's album – features his favorite musical theme: puppy love. 'I love singing about love,' Justin told *Twist* magazine. 'That's what a lot of girls like listening to, and that's what I like to write.' With the single scheduled for an April 2009 release, it would soon be time to put some professional video production behind his youthful voice. L.A. Reid signed off on a $50,000 budget for a video for 'One Time.' But recording the song in the studio was very different to making the video. For years, Justin had been making videos on his mom's home camera, but this was a major production with a five-figure budget. 'It was really cool going from my webcam to professional videos,' Justin said.

The 'One Time' video was actually filmed in Usher's lavish house. At the beginning, Justin and his best friend Ryan Butler are sitting in front of the television when Usher calls to ask him to look after his house. But Biebs flashes a mischievous grin when he hangs up the phone and turns to Ryan. Within seconds, he and his friend are texting everyone on their phones and inviting them to come over to Usher's house for a party. As the party gets started, boys and girls dance about the house, shooting Silly String all over the place. But Justin doesn't seem interested in any of the guests – at least until one brunette in particular arrives and smiles at him. Justin spends the rest of the video singing to her. The lucky girl and Justin hang out by the pool, rocking back and forth and sitting close as the party spins around them. It seems like the perfect series of moments as he confesses how much she means to him, promising that he will give her 'everything' she needs. Still, all great nights have to end, and Justin's love interest checks her watch and leaves the party. But she just can't resist smooching him on the cheek before she departs. Now Justin sits with a wistful look on his face thinking about his girl. As he stands up to rejoin the party, he turns to see Usher wondering how and why so many teens are having so much fun in his house. Justin raises his arms to the camera and runs away with a laugh as Usher shakes his head in a comedic finish.

The video didn't immediately generate the level of anticipation that Usher and Reid had hoped for. Sure, the song was catchy, but Justin deserved a greater spotlight given his talent and appeal. So, Braun and the team returned to their favorite promotional channel: YouTube. By summer 2009, when the video was posted online, Justin's subscriber total stood at a whopping forty million fans. 'One Time' debuted at ninety-five on the Hot 100 in late July, and soared upward from that point on. As MTV and other media outlets were looking to capitalize on the online sensation, Justin's star was rising fast.

Above: *The next Michael Jackson? Justin proves he's got the moves at NYC's Rockefeller Center and LA's Nokia Theater respectively.* ***Right:*** *Sittin' pretty: Justin in a reflective mood while visiting SIRIUS XM Studio in New York, March 2010.*

Now that Justin had put out his first solo single, it was time to release the album. Surely it featured other songs that fans would want to move their feet to. Among his eight songs, Justin was extremely excited about one tune in which he shared a duet with Usher. Usher had recorded guest vocals on the hit 'First Dance.' 'It was really amazing. I never would have guessed that I would be able to do collaboration with Usher.' Justin described the duet as 'a slow groovy song that people can dance to,' so it was just a matter of time before the song in question found a global audience. 'People don't hear it and think, "Oh, it's a little kid's record,"' said Braun. 'He's a young kid who sings with a lot more soul than he should.'

Justin couldn't wait to get his album out into stores. 'It's gonna be a fun album,' he told *MTV News* upon its release. 'It's a lot about love and teen love and what would be in my world.' He revealed that the album isn't just a bunch of songs about girls; it also touches on some deeper subjects that he hopes will allow other teens to relate to his music. 'There's a lot of stuff that's not just about love. There's songs that teens can relate to, as far as parents not being together and divorce,' Justin said. 'And just stuff that happens in everyday life. There's a lot of kids my age [and] their whole album [is] "Everything is perfect."' The singer noted that in his world, the outlook isn't *always* sunny. 'Real life isn't perfect,' he said, 'so my album kind of portrays that. You just have to make the best of what you have.'

The album would be released on 17 November 2009, but the pressure was on. How would *My World* do? Would the critics be accepting of Justin's first album? And most importantly, would his YouTube fans be accepting of Justin's transition from online icon to Usher's protégé?

Biebermania

'It's like Beatlemania.
Mass hysteria. Loud screaming,
crying, passing out. It's amazing.'

– Ryan Good, swagger coach

It wasn't long before Justin heard his voice on the radio for the first time, which proved to be yet another memorable experience. 'The first time, I was in Atlanta, I was driving with my mom,' he said. 'I was in the car, and we heard it come on. We were really excited. It kind of seemed like everything I was working for was coming together. It was good.'

When *My World* was released in November 2009, everyone at Island Def Jam had their fingers crossed that Justin's album would be cherished by millions of fans worldwide. Justin certainly had full confidence that his music would soar to the top of the charts, not least because of the talented professional team surrounding him. 'I've been working with Tricky [Stewart] and The-Dream,' Justin said. 'I've worked with Bryan-Michael Cox, Johntá Austin. I've worked with a bunch of other people. I worked with The Movement, The Clutch. A lot of good producers.'

His songs were well-penned and highly personal. It seemed that he had a natural ability to reach out and move his audience, especially through the tracks that he'd helped write. 'Most are about love and stuff that girls can appreciate, but I also co-wrote a song called "Down to Earth" [with with the assistance of Midi Mafia and the Jackie Boyz]. It's a ballad about the feelings I had when my parents split up and how I helped my family get through it. I think a lot of kids have had their parents split up, and they should know that it wasn't because of something they did. I hope people can relate to it.'

Singing about his parents' divorce wasn't easy for Justin, but he found that music helped him express his feelings about life's most difficult obstacles. Another song he helped write, 'One Less Lonely Girl,' also showed Justin's sensitive views about love and relationships. 'I think it's really important [that] these girls have something so they can be one less lonely girl,' he told *MTV News*.

From the moment the album was announced, Justin's manager Scooter Braun knew that Island

Justin records his vocal for 'We Are the World,' a charity record made in support of Haitian Earthquake Relief that featured numerous other A-list artists, February 2010.

Def Jam had to be smart about how they marketed the talented teen. Given that Justin's more personal songs had a way of touching individuals who heard the lyrics, offering fans the chance to meet Justin seemed like a great way to promote the forthcoming album, and with this in mind, Braun and his team arranged a contest that was certain to increase the buzz and record sales. They would give one lucky fan an opportunity to meet Justin one-on-one and have him perform live at the winner's home.

Weeks before the album's release, Justin signed onto Twitter and announced that CDs of *My World* would feature golden tickets. Similar to the famous tickets that Willy Wonka gave to several fortunate children allowing them to visit his mysterious factory in the classic children's book *Charlie and the Chocolate Factory* by Roald Dahl, Justin's golden tickets would provide one lucky winner with the prize of a lifetime: a private concert in his or her backyard.

'IT'S TRUE!!!' Justin tweeted on his profile. 'There will be GOLDEN TICKETS in some of my albums . . . U find the right album you get a PRIVATE CONCERT for u and your friends!!!'

> 'It was definitely a struggle to finish the song. But I really didn't want to let my fans down and they were looking for a show so I had to give it to them.'
> – Justin Bieber

Scooter Braun's other plan was to release *My World* as two separate albums. 'The word is getting out 2day,' Justin again posted on his Twitter page. '*MY WORLD* is going to come out in 2 Parts. Part 1 is Nov 17th [2009] and Part 2 will start Valentines Week next year.' Even better, fans would have the chance to win golden tickets in both of the albums, so someone out there would have an early Christmas present in November, and someone else would get the best Valentine's Day gift of all time when the sequel debuted. When the album was released, fans frantically searched for the golden tickets, each hoping against hope that maybe they would be the fortunate person who earned that special performance. It turned out that Lilly, a delighted Biebette from Phoenix, Arizona, won the first prize. Justin stayed true to his word. He flew to her hometown and performed live at a private party for her and her friends. And Lilly is not the only fan girl to catch the attention of her favorite guy. Back in 2009, Tricia Matibag, a lucky tenth-grader from Ottawa, Canada, won the chance to hear Justin call out her name on the red carpet at MTV's Video Music Awards. 'I was so happy!' Tricia told *MTV News*. 'I called my best friend, because she is, like, a fan. She was just at my house, and I was screaming really loud. I love him, and it made my entire year.' Like so many other girls, Tricia recognized in Justin a kid like herself; but blessed with rare talent and opportunity. 'I love that he's just a normal guy that came from Canada like me and his dream came true. Also, he's really cute and an amazing singer,' she said.

Debuting at Number Six on the *Billboard* 200, *My World* sold more than 137,000 copies in its first week alone. In less than one month, *My World* was certified gold in the United States on 14 December 2009 and achieved platinum status on 8 January 2010. The record went on to sell more than one million copies in the United States in its first three months. Fans helped Justin make music history, as he became the first musician to have an incredible seven songs from a debut CD make *Billboard*'s Hot 100 chart. In addition to the album, Justin recorded two other tunes at the same time: a romantic version of 'One Less Lonely Girl,' in which Justin sings the lyrics in French (which he learned at a French immersion school at a young age; it is also his grandparents' first language) and a second unreleased song (later featured on iTunes) called 'Common Denominator,' which was co-written and produced by Lashaunda 'Babygirl' Carr.

But Justin's work was far from over. Now it was time to get out on the road and meet his fans.

Left: *Sean 'Diddy' Combs, Justin and Sean Kingston perform together onstage during the Help for Haiti benefit concert, Miami, February 2010.* **Right:** *Justin indulges in some hand to fan action while performing live on* The Early Show.

After the release, Bieber went on a very hectic radio and television promotional spree and a concert tour of Canada. Justin found himself jetting off all over the world. The young man who'd only taken his first vacation two years prior was now a major name in millions of households. Among his most noteworthy appearances, Justin visited *The Today Show*; more than 2,000 people arrived to see his short performance outside the studio in the middle of Manhattan. It was the largest crowd of any act the television show promoted in 2009. He would also visit *Ellen*, *Live with Regis and Kelly*, *Good Morning America*, *Lopez Tonight*, *The Wendy Williams Show*, and a score of other events, all within just a few weeks. A short time later, he even got the chance to join Fergie, Dick Clark, and Ryan Seacrest as a headline performer at the thirty-eighth annual 'New Year's Rockin' Eve' party in New York City. Still, even though his name and face were being broadcast into millions of living rooms, Justin found a way to remain extraordinarily humble and mature for someone of such a tender age. 'It's been such an amazing experience coming from a little town in Canada and to have it evolve to what it is today. So I'm very blessed,' he said.

> 'Three years ago I started a YouTube page in my little town of 30,000 people. Now I have my second album coming out and I am living my dream.'
> – Justin Bieber

After five live shows in Canada, Justin would become the opening act for his new friend Taylor Swift on the UK leg of her Fearless Tour. The two had met after Swift, a very prominent and talented teen musician herself, had become aware of Justin's music and even made his signature tune 'One Time' a theme song on her tour diary video on YouTube. 'It was so funny, because I heard about it from a fan,' Justin said of Taylor's appreciation of his song. 'I watched it and it was hilarious. She was mouthing the words. I made a video in response to hers.' In fact, Justin's response to her video was a recording of his song 'Favorite Girl,' which now has more than 9.5 million views.

Justin was only supposed to be a part of the tour for two days in London. However, his performance ended up overshadowing the gifted country singer's, after Justin hurt himself onstage during the second show. 'We were in London. I was performing at Wembley, which was an honor. I got to perform; I was opening for Taylor Swift. There was a little dip in the stage. And I was running full tilt, and I hit the little dip and I twisted my ankle. I finished the song. We ended up going to the hospital and I fractured my foot. I had to wear a boot for four weeks.'

Though Justin would complete his performance on literally one leg, he was in serious pain and had to skip the encore. It was yet another sign that Justin is fully committed to performing for his fans, and once word of his heroic performance spread, support for him swelled even more.

After his album debuted, he admitted that fame was new to him and that he was still getting used to hearing his name shouted and the screams that followed him wherever he performed. 'I'm getting more used to it every

Justin with his mentor Usher and friend Taylor Swift – whom he supported on her UK tour – backstage at Madison Square Garden, December 2009.

day,' he said while attending the Super Bowl in Miami in February 2009. 'It's amazing to come up here and have all the fans. It's so fun.' Still, as Justin's fame grew, there was now a new concern: fan safety whenever he made an appearance. Justin can certainly draw a crowd.

While promoting *My World*, he was repeatedly forced to cancel certain appearances by his promoters and even the police. The worst example of a breakdown in fan security occurred in 2009 at Long Island's Roosevelt Field Mall, where Justin was on his way to greet fans. That morning Justin tweeted, 'On my way to Roosevelt Field Mall in Long Island, NY to sign and meet fans!! I'm pumped. See u there!' No one could have anticipated the reaction to this information. More than 3,000 screaming fans showed up to catch a glimpse of their hero and nearly caused a riot. It was so bad that people were in danger of falling over the second-storey railing from so much pushing and shoving. More than thirty-five units from the Nassau County and Garden City police departments reported to the mall to help with crowd control. Five fans were sent to hospital after being trampled by others. Due to the hysteria, the Long Island police arrested Island Records' senior vice-president, James A. Roppo, and Justin's manager Scooter Braun for reckless

'[Taylor Swift] makes all the girls and even the guys relate to her, because she tells stories that actually happened. Her songs are amazing.'
– Justin Bieber

endangerment and not 'sending a timely message on Twitter' to inform fans that the event had been cancelled, as they had been instructed to do.

Still, Justin can't just stop showing up to greet his fans. His devotion and message are too important. At just sixteen years old, the young Canadian has a heart of gold and clearly strives to make the world a better place, telling *Seventeen* magazine that he aims to have his own charity by the time he's seventeen. *My World* brims with Justin's idealism. In an interview with the British magazine, *Bliss*, Justin stated that, if he had the opportunity, he would try to help protect the environment – 'I would ask everyone to turn off the electricity for a day to save power' – and confessed that a perfect day in his perfect world would include a few hours spent playing hockey and bowling with friends. In addition, Justin said that he would want to make sure that no one went to bed hungry and that everyone had the ability to take care of their family. In two words, Justin expressed his concern about one of the world's most pressing problems. 'Ban poverty,' he said.

'Having Barbra Streisand on [one] side of me, and Celine Dion on [the other] was really great . . . Snoop Dogg was in the back. The experience was out of this world.'
– Justin Bieber

Justin's awareness of a major social issue like poverty reflects his commitment to helping out the less fortunate. For this reason, he decided to participate in one of the biggest social and musical projects of 2010, a charity re-recording of 'We Are the World' in support of Haitian Earthquake Relief. In addition to Justin, eighty-one of music's most well-known artists collaborated to recreate the 1980s song dedicated to stamping out poverty in Africa. The new line-up of artists included Kanye West, Nick Jonas, Celine Dion, Rob Thomas, Wyclef, Barbra Streisand, Tony Bennett, Snoop Dogg, Jamie Foxx, Carlos Santana, Melanie Fiona, Enrique Iglesias, Miley Cyrus, Faith Evans, and Gladys Knight.

'Having Barbra Streisand on [one] side of me, and Celine Dion on [the other] was really great . . . Snoop Dogg was in the back,' Justin told Katie Couric. 'The experience was out of this world.'

Of course, Justin's experience in the star-studded choir was unique. He was originally supposed to sing a line in the middle of 'We Are the World,' but during the recording Lionel Richie was so impressed with Justin's delivery that he asked him to try singing the song's signature opening lines, which ultimately appeared on the final recorded version. 'I had this line in the middle of the song,' Justin explained, 'and Lionel [Richie] said, "I want you to sing my lines. Can you sing the first couple [of] lines?" And I was like, "Yeah, I can do that." So I sang the first couple [of] lines and he was like, "You did great," and so we kept it.'

The song received its world premiere during coverage of the opening ceremony of the Vancouver Winter Olympics on 12 February. Millions of people around the world got the chance to hear Justin's opening vocal; it was a moment when Justin stood out, even in the elite company of so many superstars.

In just a few short months, Justin had gone from uncertainty about how his album would turn out to becoming one of the music world's most promising young faces. Still, Justin recognizes that he wasn't doing this alone. In addition to some very talented producers and his ever-supportive mother, he could rely on his best friends. 'My friends are so excited for me. They've been supportive since day one. I'm really thankful.' With everyone behind him and his star rising, Justin would soar to new heights with the release of the second part of his debut album.

Justin 2.0

'It's almost like he'd already mapped out in his mind what his story could be, and it's up to us to navigate him.'

– Usher Raymond

At just fifteen years old, the immensely talented Justin Bieber had already performed for the President of the United States and found himself the guest of honor on many of television's most watched talk shows. He was surely on top of the world after his first trip to Europe to open for Taylor Swift (despite the fractured foot), and after seeing *My World*'s sales go platinum. But just when it seemed that 'Bieber Fever' couldn't get any more contagious, the global phenomenon reached an entirely new level of extreme in March 2010. The release of the second half of Justin's album, *My World 2.0*, saw the young star go supernova. Fans couldn't wait to get their hands on part two of Justin's remarkable debut. By the day before its release, more than one million copies had been pre-ordered in the US alone. After the stroke of midnight on 19 March 2010, Justin typed a special thank-you message to his most supportive fans on Facebook: 'MY WORLD 2.0 is here!!! Thank you all for changing my life. ENJOY.' Justin was not exaggerating his fans' impact on his life.

Within minutes of the album's release, Justin had officially dethroned the Jonas Brothers as the most beloved performer of the young adult market, after the trio of brothers had dominated for more than three years. And just as with his first album months prior, Justin's songs were making history. *My World 2.0* debuted at the top of the *Billboard* Hot 100. This made him the youngest male solo artist to reach that level of success since 1963, when his idol Stevie Wonder achieved the same feat. To make the moment even more exciting for the young man with the mischievous sense of humor, his debut actually created a little bit of a rivalry between him and his mentor Usher Raymond. Both artists released new albums in March. Usher's release knocked Justin off the top spot after the teen's first week in the charts. But Justin soon returned the favor, with *My World 2.0* bumping Usher's platinum-selling *Raymond V Raymond* down the chart just one week later. (It wasn't the first time that Usher and Justin had gone head-to-head, as they frequently play

Portrait of the artist as a young man: Justin poses backstage at a Biz Session to promote My World 2.0, *London, March 2010.*

one-on-one basketball. When filmed for a *Today Show* appearance in December 2009, Justin beat Usher in a game by five points. It's unclear if Justin will play Usher again in front of cameras – he'll want to make sure he can keep his bragging rights.)

Expectations were certainly high for this second half of the album, and sales were just one measure of how successful it would become. Fans naturally purchased *My World 2.0* because they loved the songs from the first part of the album. But now he'd have to meet some pretty lofty expectations in order to outdo his breakthrough of only months prior. Could Justin be about to disappoint fans and critics alike with his sophomore effort? Of course not.

Reviews of *My World 2.0* were very strong, as should be expected given Justin's incredible talent and world-class production team. Both adoring fans and professional critics couldn't get enough of the album's catchy lead singles, 'Baby,' 'Somebody to Love' and 'Eenie Meenie,' which were all described by *Billboard* as songs 'hardwired for Top 40.' In the same review, journalist Monica Herrera also praised Justin's maturation as an artist. 'The sixteen-year-old's follow-up to last November's *My World* shrewdly elevates him from a fleeting teen phenom into an evolving pop artist,' wrote Herrera.

'I wanted to do something that was a little bit more R&B [on *My World 2.0*] and that could reach out to everyone. I just wanted to be able to show my vocal abilities.'
– Justin Bieber

With mountains of praise for his performances and a second chart-topping album, Justin was certainly set to experience even more attention than he had in recent months. Now the question was: would he be up to the challenge of even more fame and public scrutiny while keeping up with his teenage responsibilities? 'It's kind of hard to balance school and work sometimes,' Justin said of his increasingly hectic schedule. But it was only about to get crazier for him. Who would have thought that his face would appear on the covers of both *People* and *Rolling Stone* in the same month? In addition, he was invited to appear on *The View*, the 2010 Kids' Choice Awards, *Nightline*, *American Idol*, and *The Late Show with David Letterman*. But no appearance would compare to what came next. Justin soon landed one of the most sought-after musical gigs in the world, winning a slot on *Saturday Night Live*. On 10 April 2010, Justin appeared as the late-night comedy show's featured musical guest. In the process, he joined a very prestigious group of artists – including Taylor Swift, fellow Canadian Avril Lavigne, the Jonas Brothers, and Hanson – who performed live on *SNL* before their twentieth birthdays.

In May Justin also had the chance to discuss his album and success on *The Oprah Winfrey Show*. On the day of his Oprah appearance, there was another special invitation in the works for his trip to Chicago, where the 'Queen of Talk' tapes her show. Justin was invited to throw out the first pitch at a Chicago White Sox baseball game. 'Just finished Oprah rehearsals, and I'm throwing the first pitch at the white sox game,' Justin tweeted while visiting the 'Second City.' 'Let's go!' A natural athlete since his years in Stratford, Justin was certainly up to the task of tossing a strike from the pitcher's mound to the catcher's mitt. Before running onto the field, he snapped a few pictures with the team mascot in his custom-made Bieber jersey printed with the number ten. Then he jogged to the mound while fans cheered and danced in their seats to Justin's hit track 'Baby,' which was echoing throughout the stadium. On the mound, Justin eyed second base to 'check' the imaginary runner's lead. Then he threw a rising fastball that tailed outside of the strike zone. No, it wasn't a strike, but none of the Biebettes in attendance seemed to care. At worst, it showed that Justin has a very strong arm.

Rival schools: Justin and the Jonas Brothers attend the Fifty-Second Annual Grammy Awards.
Justin has since replaced the Disney-sponsored trio as the most beloved performer of the young-adult market.

The excitement of a day at the ball park didn't end there for Justin. While the pop icon watched the game from a private suite with friends, a player hit a foul ball toward Justin's seat in the third inning. At the same time, an eighteen-year-old White Sox fan named Alex Rittel jumped to try and catch the ball. Unfortunately, the ball bounced off Rittel's hand and plopped right into Justin's seats. Disappointed, the young White Sox fan turned back to the game. That's when his fortunes changed. Justin decided to reward Rittel for his attempt to catch the ball. Generously realizing that the fan would get more enjoyment out of the souvenir than he would, Justin flipped the ball to Rittel moments later.

> 'I'm the same kid I always was . . . there is just a little more pressure.'
> – Justin Bieber

'I jumped up and tried to grab it, but it tipped off my fingers and went into [Bieber's] suite,' Rittel said. 'I was like, "Oh, man, that's a bummer." Then, the next thing I know, he walks up to me and says, "Here you go, man."' Rittel asked Justin to sign the ball. Always willing to help out a fan, Justin found a pen and naturally obliged. Not only would a baseball signed by Justin make the fan's day, but his luck and popularity would only improve when he returned to school the next day. 'I took the ball to school . . . to show everyone,' Rittel said. 'So many girls were jealous. So many girls.'

But no matter how loud and exciting it was in Comiskey Park that day in Chicago, no appearance could ever quite compare to Justin's first trip to New Zealand just weeks prior. On 27 April 2010, police security was extremely tight at Auckland International Airport. That night, a frenzied army of restless teenage girls awaited Justin's arrival on Kiwi soil. Many of them – hoping to get a

glimpse of their favorite star – had arrived in the morning, even though Justin was not due until late in the evening. Over time, more and more came, many holding homemade posters bearing swooning messages like 'Marry Me Justin' and 'I Want to Be One Less Lonely Girl.' Every now and then, the security doors would swing open as the catcalls of more than 500 excited young ladies echoed throughout the airport. While they waited, many of them shared stories and talked about how cute and talented Justin is amongst themselves and with local reporters. And who could blame them? After several hours and numerous false sightings, 'Bieber Fever' reached breaking point when Justin sauntered through the security doors to the incredibly loud collective scream known as the 'Bieber Scream.' 'I [get] some pretty loud screams,' Justin said. 'I don't know why. You'd have to ask them. I don't know what about me they like. But I'm glad they do.' It's obvious why they scream so loudly. His note-perfect tunes and teen-dream lyrics continue to capture the hearts of millions of young women.

Still, the 'Bieber Scream' has quickly become one of the most powerful noises on earth when unleashed at maximum force by an ecstatic collection of Justin's most enthusiastic fans. If you find yourself in close proximity to Justin, you'll know the true meaning of the 'Bieber Scream.' In fact, one local Kiwi reporter couldn't believe how loud Justin's fans could squeal, and for such a long period of time. 'Man could they scream. They did so for a good hour,' said RadioLIVE correspondent Angus Bennett. 'There were, I reckon, nearly 1,000 young teenage girls that made their way to Auckland Airport last night. And every time a door opened there at Auckland International Airport terminal the place exploded with high-pitched screams and squeals as fans sort of worked themselves into a frenzy waiting for this shaggy-haired Justin Bieber.' But, ringing ears and hoarse throats aside, the sight of Justin is worth it for the fans. There's not a Biebette who'd care about not being able to speak or hear properly the next day so long as they caught a glimpse of him.

**'Those girls are crazy . . . But they're awesome.'
– Justin Bieber**

Although Justin expects to hear loud screams wherever he goes, he certainly wasn't prepared for what awaited him upon his arrival in New Zealand. That night in Auckland, as word spread of Justin's arrival, airport security was no match for the swarm of fans who unleashed that rousing Bieber Scream and frantically stormed the singer's entourage. The tweens shoved and shouldered police officers to try and get close to him. A few fans were so consumed by Biebermania that they knocked down Justin's mother, who was innocently escorting her son on his first trip to New Zealand. Several fans hyperventilated from the excitement and needed treatment from on-hand medics. Others fainted and missed the aftermath, when a few admirers were trampled during the ensuing melee in the parking lot as Bieber's private black SUV drove away from the hysterical crowds. One fan even nabbed Justin's favorite purple Yankees hat off his head (and later held it

The boy wonder down under: Justin photographed during a promotional visit to Sydney, Australia, April 2010.

for ransom online) while police tried to ensure the star's safety. In response to the feeding frenzy at Auckland International Airport, Justin signed onto Twitter the next morning and pleaded for restraint from his fans. 'Finally got to New Zealand last night. The airport was crazy,' he wrote on his message board. 'Not happy that someone stole my hat and knocked down my mama. Come on people, I want to be able to sign and take [pictures] and meet my fans but if you are all pushing security won't let me.'

'I didn't know that a piece of paper with my name on it could mean so much to these kids.' – Justin Bieber

That same morning, police had become so concerned about public safety and a potential repeat of the scenes at the airport that, much to his disappointment, they forced Justin to cancel his scheduled public performance – a major letdown for the more than 4,000 teenage fans who had waited all night to see his first Auckland concert. Though precautions had been taken to prepare for his arrival, police cited a lack of parental supervision as final justification in canceling the show. 'There were a number of parents down there [but] I would question why there weren't a larger number of parents,' Auckland deputy police commissioner Dave Owens later explained. 'We had twelve-, thirteen- and fourteen-year-olds [alone] at three and four in the morning. They were being crushed up against the barrier.'

Of course, similar reports of Justin Bieber-inspired hysteria have been reported worldwide since he began touring. The incident in New Zealand was yet another example of Justin's growing celebrity on the international music scene and the incredible emotions he generates. In Australia,

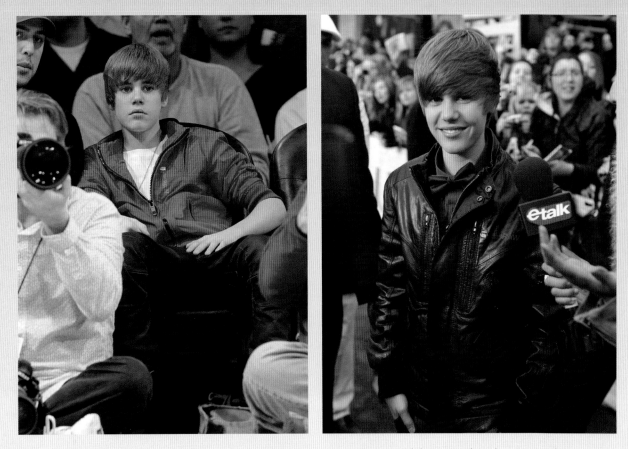

Left: *A keen athlete himself, Justin watches a game between the Denver Nuggets and the Los Angeles Lakers, Los Angeles, February 2010.* **Right:** *On the red carpet at the 2010 Juno Awards, Saint John's, April 2010.*

just weeks prior, Justin apologized when ten fans were sent to hospital after suffering injuries caused by a wild scuffle during a free concert he put on in Sydney. Similar stampedes of hundreds of fans have been reported in New York City, Paris, and Los Angeles. But the New Zealand event was the most remarkable.

His New Zealand trip also created headlines when the reported hat thief, a teenager named Emah Hira Matiu, told MTV that she was holding his favorite hat for ransom. 'I reached my hand through a massive crowd of screaming teenage girls and big-ass police guys and took it right off his head. Then shoved it down my shirt . . . got trampled . . . and then I ran away.' That evening Matiu sent Bieber a Twitter message to tell him that she had a pretty simple demand for his hat's safe return: for Justin to give her a hug. 'I do know that I have technically stolen it,' Matiu said in an attempt to justify her naughty behavior. 'But he's a celebrity and this is what you get for being famous . . . kinda comes with the deal . . . we didn't mean to upset him, all we wanted was a hug.' Eventually, Matiu decided to give back Justin's favorite hat. An unhappy Justin sent a message to the fan on Twitter: 'Sorry, u can't hold me ransom. I got my hat back. No hugs. No thanks u's. Just glad they did the right thing. I don't condone thievery!! Haha.'

> **'Sometimes I want to be just regular, just hanging out or whatever.'**
> **– Justin Bieber**

Lost in the craziness of the night, a lot of people had also forgotten that Justin's poor mother had been knocked to the ground during the rumpus. Luckily she was fine. The evening of the incident, she tweeted that she was okay after her fall. 'Thanks for all ur support!! I'm ok thank you!!!' she wrote. The experience with his mother's fall was a small reminder that Justin is still just a young kid, and that he needs support and help from adults in order to get his work done. Even though he is old enough to drive, he recognizes that the influence of mentors and older handlers who care about his safety and success has helped him grow up and mature much faster. 'I am with adults all day,' Justin said of his growing entourage. 'It's fun sometimes, but sometimes I'm like, "No, I want to hang out with my friends my own age." But at the same time, it makes me mature a little faster. I think I'm still immature sometimes, but I try not to think I'm hot stuff.'

In charge of Justin's safety is Kenny Hamilton, a bodyguard who watches the teen's every move. Not only does he ensure that young girls don't tear Justin apart when he makes a public appearance, but he also makes sure that Justin doesn't misbehave or get too much of an ego. During an incident when Hamilton heard Justin call one of Jay Leno's cameramen 'dumb,' the bodyguard privately scolded the teen and told him to act more professionally. In addition, Justin's manager says that the young star isn't immune from the same punishments handed out to any other teen in North America. 'He can get grounded like a normal kid,' said Scooter Braun. 'Get his computer taken away.'

'I'm going to help him become a good adult. If he's a good man, then he should be able to handle being a celebrity as a man. If the talent's still there, the talent's there.'
– Scooter Braun

Nonetheless, accounts of Justin's misbehavior appear to be isolated incidents. According to his mentor Usher Raymond, Justin has the poise and maturity of someone who has been in the music business for years. 'It's like Justin has already been here before,' Usher said. 'Although he's sixteen, when you talk to him, it's like you're talking to a well-seasoned young man. It's almost like he'd already mapped out in his mind what his story could be, and it's up to us to navigate him.'

Justin recognizes that there needs to be a lot of give and take in his relationship with his team. An independent, carefree kid, he still has that rebel urge to disobey authority from time to time. 'I kind of give people a hard time, because I want to be me, I want to be Justin,' he said. Even though he is the youngest person in the production, he is the star and has earned the right to put his foot down from time to time. 'They respect me enough to let me make my own decisions.'

As Justin has been able to gain more control of his career and mature while on the road, fans and press have taken notice of his pleasant personality and his private interests. Every day many journalists try to get the newest scoop on Justin's world. They want to better understand where he continues to find influences, especially in music. 'My inspiration is, on a music level, Michael Jackson,' Justin said, hinting at his sadness about his idol's recent death in 2009. 'I'm not able to see or hear any new music.'

At the end of the day, Justin is a normal teenage kid, one with growing aspirations outside of music ('I'd like to be an architect. That would be cool. I like drawing'), a penchant for junk food ('[I eat] too much candy. I like Sour Patch Kids'), and, of course, a soft spot for the girls. This latter interest seems to generate the most buzz when he's on the road. Whether flirting with Beyoncé at music awards shows or making claims about Kim Kardashian being his new girlfriend, Justin says that he's willing to date anyone from fans his own age to women more than twice as old. But, hopeless romantic that he is, even Justin has his limits. 'Above forty is a little too old for me,' he smiled.

7

Ladies' Man

'I haven't been in love yet.'
– Justin Bieber

Of course, there is really only one question that matters to every young female fan with a crush on Justin Bieber. The answer: 'I don't have a girlfriend right now,' Justin confessed, sounding almost disappointed. 'But I'm sixteen. I just like to hang out with girls and stuff.' True, hope remains for every young Biebette, but there's certainly a lot of competition for this adorable teen's heart.

While his single status may keep Justin's most loyal fans happy, his experience in the media spotlight when in the company of other young celebrities has invited many gossip columnists to question his next possible move. 'He's a hopeless romantic, but he is obsessed with girls,' said his manager Scooter Braun. Rumors about Justin's love life have only added fuel to the well-oiled Hollywood gossip machine already in Bieber overdrive. The tabloids certainly work fast on assumptions.

In May 2010, rumors quickly began to swirl that Justin and Miley Cyrus were romantically linked after they had dinner at Ari-Ya Sushi restaurant in West Hollywood. The sight of the two young stars out together naturally raised eyebrows in the press. Of course, it didn't help that a mischievous Justin egged on a swarm of paparazzi by telling them that Miley was 'having fun with me.' But after the meal, Bieber admitted that it hadn't been a date on his Twitter page: 'met up with a friend tonight for some dinner . . .'

While some fans of both singers may have secretly hoped that there was a budding romance between the two, it was later revealed that they were discussing a future project, a possible duet for later this year. (Any fans concerned about a potential Bieber-Cyrus relationship should be reassured that Justin has previously said that Cyrus is 'not my type.')

In fact, anyone who is even mildly interested in Justin's views on romance should know that he hasn't ever felt an incredibly strong connection with a girl, not even the three girls who he considers to be past girlfriends. 'I haven't been in love yet,' Justin has said frankly to numerous

UnBelieveable! Justin shows Toronto how it's done onstage at the
Twenty-First Annual MuchMusic Video Awards, June 2010.

interviewers over the past year. 'I've definitely loved girls. But it's kinda like puppy love. It's not the real thing, but that's what you think at the time.' Still, that hasn't stopped women of all ages from falling for the fresh-faced teen with the toothsome smile. 'I had a lot of girls chasing me before this,' Justin said with a devilish grin. 'But now there's definitely a lot more.' Most notable, and adorable, was Justin's encounter with one of his youngest fans, a girl who won a place in the singer's heart forever.

In late 2009, one of YouTube's most viewed videos was titled '3-Year-Old Crying Over Justin Bieber.' The video, which was shot by the young girl's mother, featured Cody, a three-year-old who sits in front of the camera and cries for several minutes about how much she loves Justin Bieber. While her mother points out that Cody is too young to be crying over boys and that 'we' don't need to cry over Justin, the tot replies, 'Yes we do . . . Sometimes.' The video became so popular around the world that TV host Jimmy Kimmel invited Cody onto his show, where she got the chance to meet Justin backstage. (Others have tried to imitate Cody's video in the hope of getting their own chance to meet Justin, but no one has had similar luck.) Justin spent the afternoon with Cody and her family and gave the young fan an experience she will never forget. It was another example of how loyal Justin is to his fans.

Such an ongoing commitment to reaching out to his fans has earned him praise from members of the media. 'There's no guys out there doing what he's doing,' Carissa Rosenberg, entertainment director at *Seventeen,* told Crushable.com. 'He's young, he's cute, he can dance. His music is like a teen girl's fantasy. You want to be in his world. Not to mention he's completely utilized Twitter and YouTube to really reach his fans. He responds to girls directly. To hear from a guy who you think is super-cute directly, you're like, "Wow, this is great."'

'I haven't been in love yet but I've felt love. It's a beautiful emotion that you can't really describe.'
– Justin Bieber

Fans naturally love him for his charming features and pitch-perfect voice, but that doesn't limit the unusual antics they use to get his attention. 'The craziest thing a fan has done,' he said. 'Well, not just the fans, but there's a fan's mom that actually got a tattoo of a radio DJ's face so that she could get her daughter backstage passes to my concert, which is pretty crazy to me.' In April 2010, Justin told *People* magazine that women frequently try to follow him home. Even so, he doesn't feel threatened. 'Moms in their soccer vans don't really scare me,' he said with a cheeky laugh. He also sometimes finds himself confused when people ask him to sign unusual items. 'Someone asked me to sign a cereal box, which was really weird,' he said.

Still, no matter how much he tries to hide it, Justin is a natural flirt, a happy-go-lucky teen who enjoys having fun twenty-four hours a day and meeting as many of his celebrity crushes as possible, even if the chance encounters get him or the girl into trouble with his protective fans. One of his newest crushes in May 2010 was reality TV star Kim Kardashian, best known for the hit American show *Keeping Up with the Kardashians* and her romantic link to NFL star Reggie Bush. However, some fans weren't too pleased to learn about the supposed romance budding between Justin and the beautiful TV star. The two had met and posed together at the White House Correspondents' Dinner in Washington DC that month. Attaching a brand-new picture of himself and Kardashian to a post on Twitter, Justin jokingly wrote, 'Look it's my girlfriend @kimkardashian.' The bubbly and jovial Kim played along with his online prank, commenting on her message board, 'I officially have Bieber Fever!!!' The joke was that Justin is thirteen years younger than his make-believe girlfriend.

Left: *Justin meets his celebrity crush Beyoncé in the audience at the Fifty-Second Annual Grammy Awards.*
Right: *Justin performs with fellow teen idol Miley Cyrus during MuchMusic Video Awards, June 2010.*

But a few of the Biebettes didn't find anything funny about this online banter. Within minutes, some of Justin's two million Twitter fans lashed out and began to issue death threats against Kardashian, claiming that Justin was theirs and theirs alone. 'I'm getting death threats from your fans!' Kardashian soon wrote on his Twitter board. 'This is unBeliebable!!!'

In response, Justin had to squash the threats, calling for a quick end to such unruly behavior. 'Ladies calm down,' he tweeted. He wrote that Kardashian was 'a very sexy friend but [just] a friend. no need 4 threats. Let's all be friends and hang out often.'

It wasn't the first time that Justin had gotten himself in trouble for making a comment about one of his celebrity crushes. Closest to his heart over the years has been the very beautiful, very talented, and very married singer Beyoncé Knowles. At the Fifty-Second Annual Grammy Awards, Justin accidentally announced Beyoncé's name instead of singer Jon Bon Jovi's while onstage. 'Maybe I was trying to get Beyoncé's attention,' Justin said with a laugh. Over the past year, the starry-eyed teen has repeatedly said that he would love to do a duet with Beyoncé, and swooned about meeting her backstage on the night of his error, much to the playful disapproval of her husband Jay-Z. 'I got to take a picture with her, and Jay-Z was like, "Watch it,"' Justin laughed.

For a long time Justin has said that he's had a crush on Beyoncé since her days with Destiny's Child. Even in his childhood bedroom in Stratford, he plastered the walls with posters of the stunning diva. 'I've been totally in love with her since I was seven. She kinda broke my heart when she married Jay-Z,' he laughed.

Despite the ongoing attention devoted to his love life and success, not everyone has caught the Bieber Fever. In early 2010, Justin was the target of one of singer Ke$ha's unprovoked verbal attacks. The California-born singer and rapper said during an interview with *Maxim* magazine

Left: A vision in white: Justin works the crowd at KIIS FM's Wango Tango concert, Los Angeles, May 2010. **Right:** Signing autographs for fans after throwing a ceremonial first pitch before a Chicago White Sox game, Chicago, May 2010.

that she didn't have a high opinion of Justin. 'He's such a tiny little baby! I would've loved to push him around onstage in a carriage.'

The comments were certainly uncalled for (and Ke$ha would later apologize), especially given that Justin is always optimistic and never speaks negatively about anyone in show business. But, in fact, throwaway comments like these are the least of Justin's worries. 'The most challenging aspect of living in the limelight,' mused the teen star. 'Not being able to see my friends and family as much as I'd like to is definitely challenging. That's probably the most challenging, not seeing my best friends for so long.' The second biggest challenge for Justin is being expected to respond to criticism of his looks or his art. Luckily he can rely on his many grateful and supportive fans, who want him to do well. 'My fans are really argumentative and really supportive. If someone sends a bad message to me, they'll attack them. There's always going to be haters.' Justin never responds to people who send a nasty comment to him online. 'I just brush it off my shoulders. My fans stick up for me.'

'I'm single and ready to mingle!'
– Justin Bieber

Every loyal fan of Justin's has a different story about how they first discovered him, and nearly all of these fans, no matter where they are in the world, believe that Justin will be one of music's top performers for years to come. For Nicole Underwood and Izzy Barchi – two eighteen-year-old fans from Canterbury in the UK, who recently completed their A-level exams – Justin Bieber is the real deal.

'I first came to discover Justin Bieber on YouTube, before he was famous,' Underwood said. 'Most home videos on YouTube are very similar, but for me Justin Bieber really stood out, his voice was always in tune and he was amazing!'

Barchi had a similar experience, and claims that she is also one of the original fans who found Justin prior to his success with Island Def Jam. 'I discovered him whilst browsing YouTube and ended up watching all of his older home videos of him covering some classic R&B songs,' said Barchi. '[My] first reactions were that he had an amazing voice for someone of his age, at this point he must have only been about fourteen. His voice didn't sound like something you would expect to come from a boy so young, which was a welcome change. Not only did he sound the part, but he looked the part as well. I could see his potential in how he performed, he managed to ooze confidence but not in an arrogant way.'

'It's weird when people say, "You're only fifteen," because I know I'm only fifteen, but at the same time I think at any age you can experience love.'
– Justin Bieber

So what else is it about Justin that makes him stand out from all the other singers and performers out there? 'I think the fact he is just like any other normal teenager gives people hope that they can succeed,' said Underwood. 'I think teenage girls like him because there's finally someone their age who has become a star who is young, cool and good-looking.'

Barchi agreed, saying that Justin has distinguished himself from the hundreds of other acts out there. 'I think his popularity stems from how talented he is for someone so young and I'm sure it doesn't hurt that he's easy on the eyes! I love that his voice isn't at all generic as it has a more soulful essence, and this separates him from other teen singers. He doesn't have a lot of competition as there aren't many male teenage solo artists that spring to mind, so the fact that he is a completely unique artist weighs highly in his favor. I see him as the teen icon of my generation and I'm sure many others would agree.'

Being the icon of a generation has certainly required a lot of work, but Justin has been up to the challenge since day one. In fact, Justin's use of Twitter and open conversations with his followers – his ability to really connect with his fans – has made him stand out from other performers and changed the way popular musicians interact with the public as well. 'He's really accessible to his fans,' said Leah Greenblatt of *Entertainment Weekly*. 'He's always putting up new videos, he might tweet you back, he's not this remote superstar. You can almost track him in real time. That doesn't make him exceptional, it just makes him really representative of pop stardom now, because Lady Gaga and Ke$ha do the same thing. And because he's like this boy dreamboat, it means a lot to girls. I think it really gooses the loyalty that they have for him and the devotion.'

For young women like Barchi and Underwood, Twitter is the best way for them to continuously get up-to-date information on one of their favorite stars. 'I do have a Twitter account and one of the main reasons I made one in the first place was so I could follow Justin!' said Underwood. 'It makes him so much more real when you see his tweets, and you know that he really cares about his fans.'

Indeed, Justin really does care about his fans. But at the same time, he still feels a bit odd when so many people are screaming or chanting his name whenever he makes an appearance. Certainly he is aware of his fame and his ability to get people excited, but regardless of that, he sees himself as just a normal kid who's having fun as he goes along. 'I still feel regular. You know, sometimes it's weird that I go places and I have thousands of people waiting for me,' he said. 'But I always think, "I'm [just] Justin."'

Future Fever

*'He's definitely a priority
for me and Island Def Jam.'*

– Usher Raymond

Justin might just be a humble sixteen-year-old kid from a small town who likes girls, sports and engaging in the occasional prank now and then. But to millions of fans around the world, including his mother, Justin is on another plane when it comes to his talent. 'I knew he would always sing, but I just didn't think it would be on this level,' his mom said. The future is extremely bright for Stratford's darling teen. He recently signed a new deal with Universal Music Group, the parent company of Island Records, which guaranteed an incredible $400,000 advance for his next album. His hardworking team began production in the summer of 2010, and rumors are swirling that it could be released around Christmas 2010.

Despite his growing wealth and the adoration of millions of loving fans, becoming a global phenomenon has not been the easiest experience for the handsome young superstar. 'Having this type of success at this age, so quick, can be very overwhelming,' his mentor Usher told *Good Morning America*. 'I'm really happy that I'm able to pull from my own experiences to help him understand how to handle it.' Needless to say, Justin faces many challenges, especially the long days on tour, in the studio, or when hitting the books. Between interviews and appearances, Justin has to study for a mandatory three hours each day. Like any other teen, he isn't pleased about the homework. 'School sucks,' he said bluntly. And, to top it off, he really only gets one day off each week, which isn't enough for an active young man with athletic interests. Always a competitor, he prefers playing basketball or skateboarding to sitting around airports or hotels all day.

At a time when he is just obtaining his driver's license and should be looking forward to his high-school junior prom, Justin is living out of hotel rooms and answering select Twitter messages from nearly 2.5 million fans on a daily basis. 'On Twitter I follow people, but I can't really keep up with them because I have all my fans and my [inbox] just gets flooded,' Justin said. 'I follow all of my fans

True Belieber: Justin on the red carpet at the Twenty-First Annual MuchMusic Video Awards, June 2010.

though.' Sure, it can be immensely stressful for a young kid to have so many people sending him messages, especially when he tries to find the time to answer all of his fans. But being loyal to his fans, Justin feels obligated to answer everyone, even if he has to stay up past his bedtime. Though it takes some time, Justin knows that a little note can make all the difference in the world, for both himself and his fans. 'People write to me and say, "I'm giving up, you're not talking to me,"' Justin said. 'I just write them a simple message like, "Never give up," you know? And it changes their life.'

For teenage fans like Izzy Barchi and Nicole Underwood, that little bit of effort really shows the difference between Justin and many other celebrities when it comes to how they treat their fans. 'I have a Twitter account and have noticed that he in fact spends a substantial amount of time tweeting,' said Barchi. 'I follow him and love the comments he makes. It makes me realize how, despite being a huge celebrity with a vast fan base, he still manages to remain humble and doesn't let his sudden popularity go to his head. His personality makes him much more approachable and it's great that he allows it to shine through the barrier that comes with being a celebrity. I have never tweeted him myself, but I enjoy reading what he has to say, it helps him become a real person, not just an untouchable celebrity.'

'I tell [Justin] like I tell any artist, either be passionate fully about what you do or don't do it at all. And understand that the perception of what you build is the reality of what they will believe.'
– Usher Raymond

When Justin is on the road, there is no formula for how he carries on his day. Sure, he shows his age from time to time when he ignores his mother's requests to clean up or sneaks in ten minutes of his favorite video game, *NHL 2010*, between concert sets. According to his mother, he and she are sometimes at odds over little things. 'No [teenager] wants to be around his mother twenty-four seven,' Pattie said. 'And no mother wants to be around her [teenager] twenty-four seven, either.'

Still, Justin regularly says that his fame has taught him to show appreciation to everyone who supports him and, more than anything, drives him to make a difference in the lives of his fans. 'I'm looking forward to influencing others in a positive way,' Justin said. 'My message is you can do anything if you just put your mind to it. I grew up below the poverty line; I didn't have as much as other people did. I think it made me stronger as a person, it built my character. Now I have a 4.0 grade point average and I want to go to college and just become a better person.'

For now, however, the college campus can wait. He looks set to graduate from high school in the near future and will press on with his soaring career. 'I think older people can appreciate my music because I really show my heart when I sing, and it's not corny,' he said. 'I think I can grow as an artist and my fans will grow with me.' And that incredible career will not just be limited to music.

In the last few months, Justin and his team have been negotiating several different film projects to suit his skills and signature look. Justin has openly said that he aspires to one day become an actor, so why not get started now? 'I definitely want to do a movie,' Justin said. 'That's something I want to get done.' It's a good thing that Justin has already spent so much time in front of the camera. For years now, the young showman has been creating videos, presenting awards onstage, and acting – as with his appearance as a guest star on Nickelodeon's *True Jackson, VP*. On April Fools' Day in 2010, Justin also assumed control of Will Ferrell's comedy website FunnyorDie. com for twenty-four hours, and renamed it after himself. 'Hey what's up internet? Guess who?' he said in the first video posted on the site that day. 'It's Justin Bieber, and I'm taking over Funny or Die. It's mine. I bought it. And now it's Bieber or Die. Anything that's not Bieber . . . dies . . .'

Left: *Hats off: Justin is all smiles despite his jet lag at Narita Airport, Japan, May 2010.*
Right: *Seeing the light: The Biebs onstage during BBC Radio One's Big Weekend in Bangor, Wales, May 2010.*

During the opening video, Justin generates a number of laughs, claiming that he pays people to let him slap them or to carry him around, and how he buys night clubs where he isn't old enough to enter and converts them into Chuck E. Cheese restaurants – a favorite location for kids' birthday parties. 'Now who's old enough?' he asks with mock-defiance. 'This is Bieber's world. You're just living in it. Bieber or Die.' Other hilarious video shorts from the day include Justin's creation of a computer screensaver in which he works on a computer and flirts with the viewer, a performance from the top of a table that ends in a tragic tumble, and an adaptation of one of YouTube's most famous videos of all time, renamed 'Bieber After the Dentist.'

> **'My whole crew, they don't really treat me like I'm a celebrity or anything. They just treat me just like a normal kid.'**
> **– Justin Bieber**

Justin clearly enjoys being in front of the camera, and his eyes are directed toward potential blockbuster films rather than the pop Disney shows and movies that have recently launched the careers of stars like Zac Efron and Demi Lovato. 'I don't want to do the Hannah Montana thing,' Justin said. Justin has spoken with producers about a potential biopic that centers on his meteoric rise to fame from poverty in Stratford. 'We're trying to set up a movie for me in the near future – it's going to be similar to the story of how I got discovered. Kinda like my own version of *8 Mile*.'

Of course, Justin also chats about who he would like to work with in the future, always returning to one of his celebrity crushes. 'I would love to collaborate with Beyoncé,' he said. 'She's

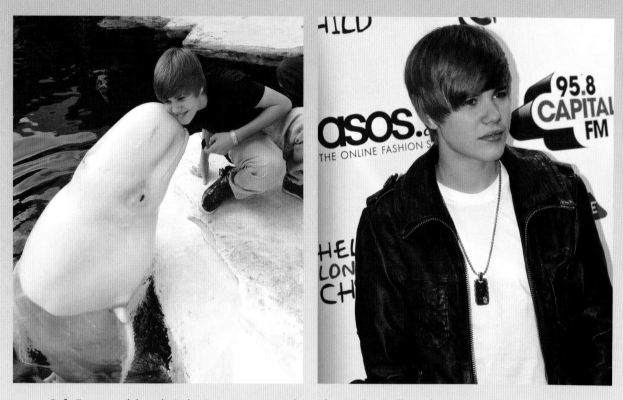

Left: *Even animals have the Bieber Fever! Justin gets up close and personal with Allua, a female beluga whale, at SeaWorld San Diego, May 2010.* **Right:** *Justin backstage at Capital FM's Summertime Ball, Wembley Stadium, London, June 2010.* **Next page:** *'I think I can grow as an artist and my fans will grow with me,' says Justin.*

beautiful.' He also finds himself thinking about who he would like to be on tour with if he could choose artists from any time in music history. 'I would want to go on tour with Michael Jackson, but I can't and it's sad,' he told Katie Couric. Above all else, Justin certainly dreams big about his future. His words ring with incredible confidence and he is absolutely sure that he can continue to make his dreams come true in the coming years. Meanwhile, the rest of his team share the same level of faith and are poised to help Justin accomplish his goals, even if it means that he has to sacrifice his own comfort in order to meet the expectations of his fans.

'The answer to me is that you help him become a man,' his manager Scooter Braun said. 'You surround him with people who don't treat him any differently. Justin rode coach today because there was no first class available and we had to get somewhere. It was no questions asked. He's been given a gift and a blessing, but that doesn't make you better than anyone else.'

When asked by Neonlimelight.com about the pressures of working with the knowledge that the immensely talented Usher Raymond is his mentor and producer, Justin said that no one puts more pressure on him than Justin Bieber does. 'I'm kind of a perfectionist, so I always like to do my best. Yeah . . . I guess there's a little bit of pressure, but I don't think he puts that on me. I think that it's just me.' If he finds himself struggling, Justin knows that he always has Usher to back him up. Given that Usher experienced a similarly early and successful career, the legendary R&B singer will be the perfect guide for Justin. '[Usher] just basically told me to keep my head on straight. Make sure to stay grounded. I mean, he's been through the whole process. He's done it all before so he's kind of coaching me. He's kind of my mentor.'

In fact, the only concern that anyone seems to share about Justin's future rests on the fact that he is undergoing puberty and his voice is becoming deeper. Given that his voice is breaking, it has impacted his ability to carry certain notes from his signature hit 'Baby' in their original key. 'Some of the notes I hit on "Baby" I can't hit anymore,' Justin said. 'We have to lower the key when I sing live.' Still, Justin remains extremely optimistic and knows he's got the talent and the backing to hit the necessary notes when the time comes. 'It cracks. Like every teenage boy, I'm dealing with it and I have the best vocal coach in the world.' Justin also ignores people who think he's just part of a larger teen fad that comes and goes every few years. 'There's more people that like me than there are who hate me, so I kind of brush it off,' he said. 'People say, "Oh, people just like him because he's pretty." Or the funniest one: "When he goes through puberty, he's not going to be a good singer anymore." How does that make sense when we've seen people like Michael Jackson and Usher and Justin Timberlake and all these famous singers do it?' He certainly raises a good point, and he knows that he has the time, the passion, and the team to stay on top of the world no matter how much his voice changes.

'Michael Jackson was able to be young and influence a wide variety of people so, you know, that's what I would wanna be like.'
– Justin Bieber

Even if there is some bad press now and then, it won't stop Justin from being a kid and having a good time. When he turned sixteen years old, he flew thirty of his friends out to Los Angeles for the Sweet Sixteen party of a lifetime. During the extravaganza, Justin sumo-wrestled with Young Money upstart Lil Twist and learned that Usher was buying him his first car. 'I'm only sixteen once,' Justin said. 'I got to live like it.' And live like it he will, when he has the time. Still, as someone who likes his free time, his sixteenth year on earth will be another spent on planes, in hotels, in concerts and in interviews.

Justin began his first full North American tour in June 2010 with his friend Sean Kingston, who is prominently featured in the immensely popular *My World 2.0* single, 'Eenie Meenie.' The tour was initially set to launch on 23 June at the XL Center in Hartford, Connecticut and travel through more than forty cities before wrapping up in Allentown, Pennsylvania on 4 September. However, in light of Justin's immense popularity and his love of performing for his fans, many more shows were added all across the country through to late December. In fact, Justin was so anxious to get out on the road and see his fans that he actually skipped the BET Awards in June, where he was nominated for Best New Artist. 'Missing everybody out in LA for the BET Awards,' he tweeted during the first Sunday of his tour. 'Just wanted to say I would have been at the awards, but this show was booked before the nominees came out, and I don't cancel shows. I would never cancel a show and let down the fans unless I had to . . .'

Even though Queens MC Nicki Minaj beat Justin to the Best New Artist prize, Justin was honored by the nomination. 'But I do wish I was there too, because I am honored to just be nominated but just goes to show that music is COLOR BLIND!! It is the universal language, and good music brings us all together . . . the way it should be.'

There will be many more award opportunities for Justin in the years ahead. But for now, the fresh-faced teen from Stratford aims to be more than a global icon. With the support of his friends and family and a wealth of experienced mentors continuing to back him in the future, the sky is the limit for this once-in-a-lifetime talent who continues to show the value of hard work when it comes to reaching your goals. 'The harder you work, the more successful you can be,' Justin said. 'This is just the beginning for me.'